Getting the Buggers into Languages

Amanda Barton

continuum
LONDON • NEW YORK

Relevant titles

Getting the Buggers to Add Up – Mike Ollerton (forthcoming)

Getting the Buggers to Behave – Sue Cowley

Getting the Buggers to Draw – Barbara Ward

Getting the Buggers to Write – Sue Cowley

Getting Your Little Darlings to Behave – Sue Cowley

Guerilla Guide to Teaching – Sue Cowley

How to Survive Your First Year in Teaching – Sue Cowley

Sue Cowley's Teaching Clinic – Sue Cowley

CONTINUUM

The Tower Building   15 East 26th Street
11 York Road   New York
London SE1 7NX   NY 10010

www.continuumbooks.com

© Amanda Barton 2003

British Library Cataloguing-in-Publication Data
A catalogue record for this book is available from the British Library.

ISBN: 0-8264-7170-6 (paperback)

Typeset by BookEns Ltd, Royston, Herts.
Printed and bound in Great Britain by Cromwell Press, Trowbridge, Wilts

Contents

Acknowledgements

My heartfelt thanks to all those teachers and PGCE trainees whose inspirational creativity has helped to fill these pages. Particular thanks goes to those teachers and pupils who invited me into their classrooms, especially Val McDonald, Nick Jones, Jane Talbot, Roberto Ruffo, Norma Horton and Kristin Watkin.

My thanks to Alexandra Webster for her patience, and to my boys – Alexander and Hugh – for keeping me laughing.

Introduction

I can still remember how I felt after my first French lesson as a pupil in a middle school in Staffordshire. Returning home to Mum, I was desperately keen to convey the excitement that I felt on having the opportunity to learn how to communicate with someone in a foreign language.

This excitement was not fuelled by having been abroad, or by the prospect of travelling abroad in the near future; our family holidays only took us as far as Blackpool or Cornwall. So, why the excitement? Was it simply the association of 'foreign' with exotic adventures that excited me, or was it an awareness that learning a foreign language would open up doors into whole new worlds? Or was it because I was a girl, and girls either naturally love languages, or are encouraged to do so?

This last possibility has come to my attention as a result of spending the last few years investigating how boys and girls approach learning languages. When I began my PGCE in Coventry, I was disappointed and surprised to find that not all pupils shared my love of languages. In spite of all my energetic cavortings in the classroom, and the long nights spent trying to produce flashcard and OHT pictures that bore some vague resemblance to town halls and sausages, many of my pupils remained uninspired, and the majority of these appeared to be boys.

Gender differences in Modern Foreign Languages (MFL) also characterized the classes I encountered during my first teaching post in a 13–18 comprehensive school in Staffordshire. The lower ability groups were composed predominantly of boys and boys seemed to prefer German to French.

Embarking on a doctoral study of gender differences in language learning gave me the opportunity to explore the issue of improving boys' motivation and performance in much more depth. Observing teachers in action, interviewing pupils and staff, and sharing effective strategies with teachers during Inset gave me a much better insight into the differences between boys' and girls' learning styles and preferences, and how these can be accommodated in the classroom. Working with pupils taught in single-sex classes also allowed me to evaluate the effectiveness of this initiative in raising achievement.

This book presents a range of effective teaching strategies that were discovered in the course of this research. They can all be easily applied in the classroom and they have all been 'tried and tested', either by me, by the teachers in my case study schools, by those who attended workshops or by PGCE students at the University of Manchester.

It is clear that the issue of boys' underachievement in MFL is still very much at the forefront of many teachers' minds. Ofsted inspection reports frequently highlight the gap in performance and recommend that appropriate measures be taken to reduce it. The GCSE statistics for 2002, shown below, reveal that, while there is still a gap across the curriculum, the gender gap is at its greatest in the language-based subjects: MFL and English.

	Boys %	Girls %
5+ Higher grades (A★–C) GCSE	46	56.6
Higher grades (A★–C) Maths	48	50
Higher grades (A★–C) Science	46	50
Higher grades (A★–C) English	46	64
Higher grades (A★–C) MFL	32	47

Raising boys' achievement in MFL is, therefore, a very real challenge for many teachers. Recent government legislation, allowing pupils to opt out of a language at Key Stage 4, has perhaps intensified the challenge. If we are to halt the threatened closure of many university language departments, and to reduce the 9 out of 10 students who currently drop a language post-16 (*Nuffield Languages Inquiry*, 2000) we need to look very closely at why pupils are demotivated and act on our findings.

Consequently, this book presents the views of pupils alongside those of their teachers. Pupils, I have discovered, are the best qualified people to comment on what it is like to learn a language in secondary school and are often able to offer insight that is as enlightening as it is amusing.

In focusing on boys' learning styles it is not, in any way, my intention to discredit the tremendous academic strides made by girls in recent years. Underachievement is by no means restricted to boys alone, and many underachieving girls share certain characteristics with underachieving boys. I hope that making languages more accessible and appealing for boys will allow them to break free of the prevailing destructive masculine stereotype that prevents them from doing well in subjects which may be associated with the opposite sex. Learning a foreign language has much to offer boys: being able to express your feelings and to communicate adeptly with others, whether in your first or another language, are skills that are integral to one's personal development and highly valued by employers.

I hope that you find something of value in this book and that it helps to generate in your pupils, regardless of their gender, the excitement that comes with learning a new language.

1 Why don't the buggers love languages?

We can only begin to plan and implement effective teaching strategies when we have considered how boys and girls perceive MFL. I would argue that pupils' attitudes to MFL play a far more important role in determining performance than they do in other subjects. There are two reasons for this:

1. The subject is not led by a factual, impersonal content but makes particular demands on the individual. Pupils need to be especially receptive and open to internalize a foreign culture and need to have empathy with speakers of the target language. Sadly, our tabloid newspapers all too often ensure that this is not the case by publishing headlines that are derogatory about our European neighbours. Headlines such as 'Huns on the run' (*Daily Sport*, 2 April 2003) are not uncommon. They frequently precede articles about sport (the headline above referred to the European Football Championship) and are likely, therefore, to impact more on boys who are often keen readers of articles about sport.

2. Pupils begin learning languages at a comparatively late stage of their personal development, at a time when attitudes are heavily shaped by their heightened sexual, and gender, awareness. It is highly likely that pupils will be reluctant to do well in a subject that is associated with the opposite sex.

This chapter provides the background to the strategies described in the rest of the book. It aims to give you a little insight into pupils' attitudes to languages and to answer questions that are frequently asked by teachers during in-service training.

Practical suggestions of how some of these issues might be tackled in the classroom are also given.

Tackling prejudice through language awareness

Boys' generally less positive attitudes to language learning have been registered by both teachers and pupils; girls, it seems, enjoy learning foreign languages more than boys.

Girls' greater preference for languages is evident even before pupils begin learning languages in secondary school; of 210 Year 7 pupils who were asked in their very first ML lesson in secondary school if they were looking forward to learning languages, 89 per cent of girls agreed, compared with 73 per cent of boys. While this does not seem to be a huge difference, it is worth noting because the gap widens progressively through secondary school. It suggests the wisdom of teachers explicitly addressing pupils' preconceptions about language learning either in primary school, or in the early stages of secondary school. Awareness-raising, focusing not merely on language acquisition skills, but also discussing the applications and benefits of language learning, could perhaps serve to dispel some of the prejudices feeding boys' demotivation, which increases steadily throughout secondary school. Pupils in primary school often have very unclear views of what they will be doing, or achieving, through learning a language.

Tackling the pupils' preconceptions or prejudices can be done in the very first few language lessons, by the means outlined below. I have selected French as this is still the first foreign language taught in schools, although the exercises can be adapted for other languages:

Step 1: The pupils are invited to write down the first words that occur to them when the word 'French' (target language) is mentioned. These are likely to include snails, garlic, wine, perfume and, possibly, the Renault Clio.

Step 2: The teacher then explores the origins of these cultural stereotypes: ask the pupils to write down why they thought of those words. It is likely that they will refer to adverts that are currently on TV. This should generate a discussion about how advertising, and the tabloids, help to construct our attitudes to foreigners.

Step 3: The teacher shows a range of adverts, clips of films, or images, and plays pieces of music associated with the French in order to show that the French can be perceived in many ways. A good advert to use here is the Stella Artois lager advert which demonstrates a sense of humour and has the script in the target language, with subtitles. A clip from the film *Amélie* can be shown to demonstrate that the French are successful film-makers. Well-known French athletes and footballers – David Ginola, Zidane, Thierry Henri – and popstars should also be included. In this way, the pupils' understanding of what being French means should be broadened.

Step 4: The teacher asks the pupils to write down a number of questions that they would like to ask a French person, explaining that they will have an opportunity to put these questions to a real French person. These are likely to include questions such as 'Do you eat snails?'

Step 5: The class is joined either by the Foreign Language Assistant, or by a native speaker drafted in from the local Higher Education Institution. (Most universities now operate a system whereby undergraduates can volunteer to help out in local schools, and this is normally co-ordinated by the students' union.) The pupils have the opportunity to put their questions to the native speaker.

Step 6: The native speaker puts their own questions about the English way of life to the pupils. By this means, pupils come to see that we all construct our own stereotypes of foreigners, and that the British are no exception to this.

Homework: Pupils go on a fact-finding mission to discover more about the French, possibly using the Internet. They are asked to find out how many people speak French and in which countries it is spoken, plus one extra 'fascinating fact about the French'. This forms the focus of the next lesson when pupils also produce a display/displays of their materials.

Step 7: The teacher shows to the class a number of French words which have become part of the English language. These could include the following:

- restaurant
- rendezvous
- foyer
- café
- rôle

The meanings of these words is discussed, along with patterns that identify the words as being of French origin, such as accents. Pupils then rehearse the French pronunciation of these words. As well as being a fun exercise, this also makes pupils aware that even though words are spelt in the same way, they are pronounced differently in French and English. Avoiding anglicized pronunciation will be of key importance when pupils take their GCSE speaking test, where many marks are forfeited for poor pronunciation of this kind.

Homework: Pupils research further French words and add to the list in the following lesson.

This kind of approach is not rocket science. It does, however, address an aspect of language teaching that is all too often neglected but which is key to shaping pupils' attitudes to the language: cultural awareness. If pupils have negative attitudes to the native speakers of the language they are being taught, or are unaware of where it is used, they are unlikely to be motivated to learn it.

It is frequently argued that examination specifications leave little time to teach cultural awareness, and that it can be taught implicitly through topics: shopping, school, eating, etc. Cultural awareness is included as a discrete section in the National Curriculum Programme of Study for MFL and boys in particular often demonstrate a great deal of interest in cultural background information. Putting the language in its cultural context makes it more alive and interesting to pupils who will otherwise see it as a fiction of your own creation. If, like me, you are not a native speaker of the languages you teach you will no doubt have experienced the curiosity and amazement on your pupils' faces when they are faced with a 'real' native speaker – you are a fraud!

Lessons of this kind also have the advantage of being perceived as more 'adult'. Adolescent pupils, like mature students, often struggle with the seemingly childish nature of being asked to learn a language from scratch. It is worth discussing with them the inevitability of having to communicate in very simple language; a university student currently studying a language *ab initio* as part of their maths, engineering or science degree through a language centre would be able to sympathize with pupils in this respect and it is well worth inviting someone in through your local students' union or university language centre.

Will boys really be boys?

Teachers frequently ask whether the physiological, hormonal and neurological differences between boys and girls can account for the gender imbalance in MFL. In other words, are girls biologically predisposed to language learning, unlike boys? There is certainly some evidence to suggest that girls' linguistic skills develop at a faster rate than boys'; baby girls generally vocalize earlier than baby boys. However, the media have tended to exaggerate these differences, glossing over the fact that scientists have yet to reach a consensus on their findings regarding linguistic aptitude.

We also know that not all boys underachieve in MFL; there are still some schools where boys continue to outperform girls across the curriculum. 'A' level examination results demonstrate that those boys who continue studying a language post-16 do extremely well.

We should not underestimate the impact of sociological and environmental factors on boys' and girls' achievement. If it is 'natural' for boys to struggle in languages, why do boys who attend all-boys' schools do better in MFL than their peers who attend co-educational schools? Numerous other factors influence pupils' achievement, not least ethnic origin and social class. The following sections analyse some of the other factors which may influence boys' and girls' differential performance.

Parents

From the earliest days of infancy, society endeavours to distinguish between boys and girls. We do this by dressing girls in pink and boys in blue and by giving girls and boys different kinds of toys. Little girls are given toys that resemble human or animal life – dolls, ponies, hairdressing models, domestic appliances – while boys are given toys that encourage movement, manual dexterity and spatial ability, such as building kits, cars and mechanical kits. A glance at the packaging of most toys will reveal not only the age range for which the toy is intended, but also the sex.

Parents have different expectations of boys and girls, and interact with them differently. A well-known psychological experiment involved observing how parents responded to a baby that was first dressed in pink, and then dressed in blue. Parents presented with the 'blue' baby went down on their hands and knees and set about playing with the baby. When presented with a 'pink' baby they placed the child on their lap and began talking to them. In this way, parents may encourage their daughters to be more communicative, and passive, while boys are encouraged to be noisier and more active.

We should also bear in mind that parents' attitudes to foreign languages are likely to influence their children's, as the *Nuffield Languages Inquiry* (2000) acknowledges. My research suggests that parents are more likely to encourage their daughters, rather than their sons, to succeed in a language. Below are some ideas for making parents more aware of the benefits of learning a language:

- Invite parents to taster classes at school. Colleagues from other subjects could also be invited, since they also sometimes convey negative views of language learning to pupils. Alternatively, parents could be invited to join their children in language classes during an open day.

- Send home a fact sheet or quiz about the target language, including questions like: in which countries, and by how many people, is it spoken?

- Issue parents with an advice sheet on how they can help their children with their MFL homework.

- Organize a languages cabaret evening or a languages open day. Pupils present short sketches both in English and the target language. Parents are served food and drink associated with countries in which the language is spoken. Local exchange associations or cultural delegations, such as the Alliance Française, Instituto Cervantes or Goethe Institut could be invited.

- Ask ALL (Association for Language Learning, the UK's largest professional association for language teachers) for a copy of their information leaflet for parents. This outlines how languages are taught and answers the question 'Why are languages important?' ALL's contact details are included in the 'Useful addresses' section at the back of the book

Primary school

Some researchers have observed how primary school reinforces the gender divide, formally differentiating between boys and girls in the register, in the cloakroom, in the dining room and through disciplinary strategies. One study has shown how boys and girls communicate differently in the playground, with boys often communicating physically by greeting each other with a punch or a push. Nine year-old boys showed very little interest in each other:

> In practically every case, the boys ignored each other as people. They displayed no personal curiosity. They did not look at each others' faces. They didn't ask personal questions. They didn't volunteer information about themselves. Conversation was confined to the technical problems of Lego design. In every essential respect, the boys stayed solitary and played by themselves.
>
> Hodson, P. in Askew, S. and Ross, C. (1988)
> *Boys Don't Cry* (Open University Press)

If we think about the basis of the GCSE subject specification in MFL – teaching pupils how to talk and write about themselves, their families, their pets, hobbies, holidays and homes – it becomes clear that we may be faced with a significant challenge. Reconstructing this raw male material into able and willing communicators in their first language, let alone in a foreign language, will obviously make great demands on teachers.

Being 'cool'

Peer pressure and image

It now seems that boys are much more susceptible to peer pressure than girls, and that the pressure operating on boys may be much more aggressive than that operating on girls. Boys are under pressure to define their masculinity through a resistance to school, and a 'cool' image is all-important. While boys may want to achieve success in class, efforts must be made to preserve their status in the peer group by appearing uninterested in academic work.

My own observation of a Year 10 boys' group provided an excellent example of the internal struggle that confronts many boys: David had produced an outstanding poster for his homework that included lots of accurate and well-written French text. The teacher praised David's work and suggested that it should be shown to the Deputy. David's response to this was to smile, evidently pleased with this commendation. However, when he realized that the rest of the class were listening the smile disappeared and he gestured to one of his peers, saying, 'No, show his, mine's crap.'

The lesson to be learned from this episode is to think carefully about how we praise boys. Public praise may be counterproductive in that it threatens to alienate a boy from his peers; this seems to be the case particularly with adolescent boys. Praise given in private, or as a quiet word, may be much more effective.

Girls, too, regard being cool as important, but their views appear to change as they mature. A recent study has revealed an important difference between boys' and girls' perceptions of 'coolness'. Three tutor groups in Years 7, 9 and 11 in the same school were asked to rate how important it is to look cool. The following responses show how many pupils thought it was important, and indicate an interesting reversal over time.

	Boys %	Girls %
Year 7	7	31
Year 9	27	27
Year 11	54	8

Claire Markham, (2002) 'Images of masculinity in secondary education', MEd dissertation, University of Manchester.

The fact that it is in Year 11, when pupils sit their GCSEs, that girls regard being cool as least important, and boys regard it as being most important, may have serious implications for boys' exam success. The challenge for the teacher is to make learning languages and 'being cool' compatible.

A cool subject or a girls' subject?

Many teachers want to know whether boys are turned off MFL because they see it as a 'girls' subject'. Most rigorous studies have found that this is not the case. The vast majority of pupils I interviewed and who completed questionnaires claimed that languages are equally important for boys and girls. However, it is uncertain whether pupils' views on this are informed by a sense of 'political correctness'; the apparent indignation with which interviewed pupils dismissed the notion of it being a girls' subject suggests this may be the case. Far more pupils were happy to admit that girls might be more likely to use languages than boys. We should also not forget that the predominance of female MFL teachers might result in the subject having female connotations for many boys.

Using languages and making them relevant

Why learn languages?

At any given moment in the school day, a classroom somewhere in the UK will be resounding with the words, 'Why do we have to learn a language?' The importance of this question, and of its receiving a valid answer, should not be underestimated. Pupils' views on whether learning a language is relevant to their own lives is widely acknowledged to be a crucial factor in creating extrinsic motivation to do well in the subject. For boys especially the question carries particular weight since they are more likely to evaluate subjects on the basis of their perceived usefulness. While girls may more readily accept the necessity of learning a language, boys' attitudes are often determined by an awareness of their relevance, as one Year 9 boy testified:

> Knowing you'll use your French in the future is important. I ain't never going to use it, so there's no point in learning.

We might endeavour to make languages more real and relevant to pupils by applying one of the following strategies:

- Organize a trip abroad. Boys are clearly more motivated than girls by the experience of being able to use the language in an authentic context. Even a day trip to Boulogne or Aachen can make a huge difference to boys' motivation.

- Where family income renders trips abroad impossible, organize an intensive language day. Many language colleges now organize such days, so it is worth contacting a local language college to see whether the enterprise could be shared. An intensive language day involves taking all pupils in one year group off timetable and exposing them to another language for a whole day. Extra teachers can be drafted in from local higher education institutions in the form of PGCE students; the day is an invaluable experience for them, and can be particularly useful if they are given the opportunity to team teach with their peers. Advisers and advanced skills teachers could also be approached via the LEA. The school canteen could be asked to serve national foods, and pupils in other year groups could be asked to prepare labels for the foods in the target language.

- Prepare a display of job advertisements that require knowledge of a foreign language. Pupils could be asked to bring in the adverts themselves.

- Invite in a guest speaker from business or industry to talk to pupils about how they use languages in their working life. 'Regional Language Networks' have now been set up by the Department of Trade & Industry. These can give access to businesses that use languages and are prepared to send representatives into school. Go to *www.languagesinto.org.uk* and follow the link to your part of the UK to find out who your Regional Officer is and how to contact your Regional Language Network.

- A 'Languages Box' also exists in university Language Departments; this lists linguists who are prepared to go into school to talk about the applications of languages and includes a PowerPoint presentation 'Why study languages?' Contact the Subject Centre for Languages, Linguistics and Area Studies at the University of Southampton if you would like a visit from a university in your region: *llas@soton.ac.uk*, telephone 023 80594814.

- Pupils prepare a videoed presentation in which they dress up as pilots, technicians, tourist information officers, lorry drivers, etc. and explain how they use languages in their jobs. The video can be shown to other classes and on Open Days in the school.

- Ensure that pupils are given sound careers guidance that does not suggest that languages are only useful if you want to become an air hostess! Pupils could take a look at the following website, created by Aston University, which offers reassuring information about careers with languages: *www.les.aston.ac.uk/langlife*.

- An excellent video has been produced by the Staffordshire Languages Group that has two adolescent presenters guiding pupils through the potential uses of foreign languages. It is only 10 minutes long and could be a useful springboard for discussion. It is called 'What's the Point?' and can be obtained from David Winter, Staffordshire Languages Group, Newcastle College, Liverpool Road, Newcastle, Staffordshire, ST5 2DF, Telephone 01782 254242, Fax 01782 717396, email *dave.winter@nulc.ac.uk*, or via the website, *staffslangs.co.uk*.

- Tell them a joke that illustrates the usefulness of languages! An example:

One day, Mother Mouse spotted an open packet of biscuits lying on one of the kitchen units. As soon as the cat had gone through the kitchen cat-flap to go into the garden she ushered her baby mice across the kitchen floor. Halfway across the floor, the cat reappeared. Quick as a flash, and using the loudest voice that she could find, Mother Mouse yelled: 'Woof! Woof!' Terrified, the cat fled back into the garden. Mother Mouse then turned to her babies and said: 'So, children, now you can see why it is always worth having a second language.'

Explaining the aims

Many pupils find it hard to understand that language learning is not merely a game, hence the frequent question 'Are we doing any work today, Miss?' This may be because languages are so unlike any other subject in that so much speaking and game-playing is involved. Many boys struggle with the abstract nature of language learning. Unlike many other subjects it offers no tangible evidence that learning has been successful: in chemistry, a chemical solution changes colour as part of a reaction; in mathematics, answers are generally either right or wrong.

It is, therefore, important that pupils are made aware of what they are learning in language lessons, and why they are doing certain activities. The practice of presenting the aims of the lesson to pupils at the beginning is promoted in the Key Stage 3 Strategy for Foundation Subjects and my own experience has suggested that boys, in particular, respond well to being informed of what they are achieving, and how they are going to achieve it. The following strategies might help:

- Write up the aims of the lesson on the board and ask pupils to read, write or memorize them as they arrive. This can be a useful calming routine and can be made into a challenge if you test pupils' memories after a couple of minutes. It is important that the aims are presented in pupil-friendly language and that they do not sound like the lesson outcomes from your lesson plan. It is helpful to think in terms of the aims being preceded by the words, 'By the end of this lesson you will be able to . . .'. This allows pupils to see that they are achieving something in language lessons.

- Throughout the lesson refer back to the aims. You might ask the pupils at the end of one activity which of the aims they have now completed. This helps the pupils to link seemingly frivolous activities, such as role-play, to serious work aims.

- One of the pupils might be nominated the 'aims manager' for that lesson and have the job of ticking off, or rubbing off, the aims when they have been met. This sort of responsibility is one that may appeal to disruptive boys.

- At the end of the lesson ask the pupils to review the aims; again, this practice is endorsed in the Key Stage 3 Strategy that advocates a plenary session at the end of each lesson. It helps pupils to see that they are responsible for their own learning, and reminds them that they have, in fact, done some 'work' during the lesson.

- Ask pupils to predict what will come up in the next lesson. This allows them to see that there is some cohesion between lessons, rather than lessons being isolated units. You might inject some fun by giving a prize or merit to the person who gives the most accurate prediction.

- For the same reason, ask pupils at the beginning of each lesson to review what was covered in the previous lesson.

- Introduce new language in a context that is relevant to pupils' lives. Ask yourself when you are planning lessons, 'Why do pupils need to know this language? What are they going to use it for?' For instance, when you are teaching hobbies and leisure-time activities, ask the pupils what they talked to their friends about when they arrived at school that morning. It is likely that they (the girls at least) will reply that they talked about what they did the night before. You can then use this as the lead-in to your lesson, explaining that it is very important to be able to have this sort of language to discuss what you do in your free time with your friends. If the pupils have penfriends or email partners abroad you can also incorporate writing a letter, postcard or email using the new language into your scheme of work.

Which languages are best?

It is sometimes suggested that the predominance of French in schools is to blame for pupil demotivation. Some research has suggested that other languages will appeal more to boys. The guttural pronunciation of German, for instance, might render it more appealing to boys when their voices are breaking; the prettiness of the Romance languages might be less attractive. TV adverts also present German in a masculine context, associating it with business and fast cars, whereas French is associated with feminine images – fine wine, small cars and fashion.

There are strong arguments for offering Spanish. It has been found to be the easiest of the three commonly taught European languages after 3 years of learning, its main advantage being its grammatical consistency (Phillips, D. and Filmer-Sankey, C. (1993) *Diversification in modern language teaching*, Routledge). If pupils perceive that the main reason for learning a language is to be able to use it on holiday, as my research suggests, then Spanish would certainly be our first choice.

It is worth reminding pupils, however, that foreign languages are not just used abroad; most students seem to think that this is the case. For this reason it is worth considering with your classes which careers would necessitate using languages in this country, thinking about scenarios in which knowledge of a foreign language would be useful, or bringing in a guest speaker from business or industry, as outlined previously.

Boys' learning styles

While we should be wary of seeing boys as a homogeneous group sharing identical learning styles, many underachieving boys seem to share features which ill-equip them for learning foreign languages. Many teachers report that they are less inclined to use language for personal interaction with each other, are poor listeners, have difficulty concentrating and may prefer active, practical modes of learning.

The following is a list of common traits identified by teachers who attended workshops. They are, as we discovered at these training sessions, equally present in female underachievers.

Common characteristics of underachievers

- disorganized

- attention-seeking

- show a tendency to minimalism (I think this is a euphemistic way of saying they communicate in monosyllables or grunts! Written work shows the same trait.)

- mobile (again, a euphemism for tearing around the class-room)
- need variety, otherwise have limited concentration
- show little responsibility for their own learning, blame others
- enjoy hi-tech work
- enjoy games
- poor at forward planning, looking at anything long-term
- enjoy creative, imaginative work
- curious about cultural background information
- appreciate a clear structure to work, clear sense of direction and progress
- appreciate rewards, reassurance, encouragement
- appreciate immediate feedback about performance and progress
- need to know that the subject has some vocational value
- enjoy competition

You may disagree with some of the features included here, or be able to add some of your own. Reflecting on the common characteristics of the underachievers that you teach is a constructive exercise for a department that is keen to raise standards and needs to be followed up by matching appropriate strategies to the characteristics. It is worth bearing in mind that we are not trying to reinforce stereotypes but analysing the ways in which pupils learn in order to make languages more accessible to them.

The teacher

It goes without saying that the teacher has a vital role to play in ensuring that all pupils are enabled to achieve their maximum potential in MFL. The following chapters focus specifically on how teaching methods might be adapted to accommodate a broader range of learning styles. We begin by looking at how not to do it. The following comic monologue could be used as a stimulus for departmental discussion of gender issues, with staff identifying how Mrs X fails to engage her male pupils.

A 'model' language lesson or 'How not to teach languages'

Mrs X arrives one fine Friday afternoon to find 11 Aardvaark waiting in the corridor for her...

Right. OK. Settle down now. Oh, Mrs Shufflebottom's been moving the desks around for that roundabout thing again. You two lads, go in and put the desks back in line will you... that's it, facing the front.
OK. In we go.
Laura, dear, could you give out the textbooks, please? Lovely, thank you.
And... Guten Tag, beisammen. Wie geht's? Mir geht's jetzt wunderbar nach der Grippe. Ich habe ein bisschen Zeit gebraucht, um mich zu erholen, aber jetzt geht's mir viel besser. Es kann sein, dass ich ab und zu etwas leiser sprechen muss, weil ich eigentlich meine Stimme nicht zu sehr anstrengen darf, aber so schlimm ist es nicht.
Und dir, Ryan, wie geht's dir?... Gut ... Nein, gooot. Siehst du meinen Mund?
Hast du was Schönes am Wochenende gemacht?... Nein...That's not going to get you too many marks in the oral is it now, Ryan?
Rachel, sag mal, was hast du am Wochenende gemacht? Mmmm... Gut...Schön. ... Prima... Kevin, Hör zu!... Wunderbar... Vielen Dank.
Gut. Now on page 72 you'll find a list of jobs and while we know that we're not all going to become translators or interpretors or even use the language at all, we do need to know all the jobs for the exam. Unemployed is there anyway, Ryan, so you're catered for. Now I want you to write down neatly what you'd say in the oral exam if you were asked about your future plans. No talking now please. Get on with it.

Ryan, you've had your chance. . . .What do you mean, why do we have to learn a language? To broaden our horizons, Ryan, and because the government says so. . . Stop doodling, please, I'm not interested in your creative expression, I'm interested in getting you through the exam!

2 Speaking

How do boys see speaking?

There is considerable research evidence to suggest that for many boys speaking is the most, and in some cases the only, enjoyable aspect of the foreign language lesson. In a learning preferences questionnaire which I distributed to 288 Year 8 pupils, speaking attracted more of the boys' 'enjoy a lot' votes than any of the other three core skills. For some boys speaking is a preferable, and easier, alternative to writing:

> I enjoy speaking. I'm not so keen on the writing because I'm not very good at spelling it, but I can speak it better than I can write it. . . .
>
> (Year 10 boy)

Personality, and particularly self-confidence, is an important factor in determining pupils' attitudes to speaking. In interviews more girls than boys expressed their dislike of speaking but what was clear was that more assertive girls were more likely to enjoy it. It is now generally acknowledged that boys' approach to learning is often characterized by risk-taking. At Key Stage 3 they may be much more willing to risk contributing something in the target language, as girls often recognize:

> (*Year 8 girls*)
> Girl 1: The boys are a lot more confident in speaking, I think.
> Girl 2: Because the girls always go, 'Oh, I don't know how to say it.' But the boys just say it.
> Girl 1: They just have a go and say it.

This sounds like an obvious statement, but it is all too easy to forget that MFL is often perceived as a frightening subject both by boys and girls, and that we may need to do some work on boosting pupils' confidence. Putting the department through a Japanese or Russian taster lesson at the beginning of the year or term can be a worthwhile exercise because it is an excellent reminder of how intimidating it is to be taught a language. Having staff feed back afterwards how they felt during the lesson – when, for instance, they were asked a question by the teacher in front of the group – can be helpful in devising strategies that are less threatening to self-aware adolescent pupils.

We cannot assume that boys' enjoyment of speaking is automatic and unconditional. Boys' interest in speaking seems to decline with age, as they become more aware of peer pressure. Speaking in pairs and groups is preferred particularly by older boys and girls who are more sensitive to their appearance in front of their peers. Boys may feel that volunteering answers to the teacher's questions may threaten their acceptance by their male peers. This was demonstrated on one particular occasion when I was observing a Year 10 all boys' class taught by a very experienced female teacher. Her whole-class questions at the beginning of the lesson were met by a wall of silence; when she tasked the boys with asking and answering the questions in pairs the response was much more positive.

A further problem that needs to be borne in mind is that speaking is often not viewed as serious work by pupils. 'Work' is understood to mean reading and writing and boys often question the point of speaking, particularly at Key Stage 4 when they no longer simply enjoy communicative pairwork exercises but begin asking for the point. The strategies described below attempt to counter these difficulties.

Create more speaking opportunities

Does the balance between teacher talk and pupil talk need to be redressed? If boys are motivated by speaking, we clearly need to ensure that they have adequate opportunities to practise their speaking skills. When boys have inadequate opportunities their inhibitions develop much more rapidly. The Year 10 boys I observed during one academic year seemed, over the year, to become much more confident speakers of French, with even the most image-conscious and reserved contributing regularly to whole-class discussions and participating in pairwork. In contrast, the Year 9 boys I observed seemed to develop inhibitions quite quickly. Several boys were heard refusing to say words in French because, they claimed, they could not pronounce them. This embarrassment was no doubt fuelled by a lack of opportunities to practise: the class were never seen involved in pair- or group-work in lessons which were clearly geared to maximize the inexperienced female teacher's control of a challenging class. This episode suggests that individual teaching style, and matching teachers appropriately with pupils so that they feel able to manage them confidently and give them plenty of speaking opportunities, is all-important.

Researchers who have monitored and compared teachers' and pupils' spoken input in language lessons have often found that teachers' oral input stifles the pupils. One group of teachers in Cleveland set about acting on their own discovery of this by incorporating more speaking practice for pupils and found that one of the results was that the boys began to take role play and group discussions more seriously (in Peck, A. (1990) 'Teacher-Talk and Pupil-Talk', *Language and Learning Journal*, 2, 5–10). It may be worth inviting your colleagues to observe you in the classroom and monitor how your spoken input compares with the pupils'.

Group- and pairwork v teacher-led question and answer sessions

Much of the Cleveland teachers' speaking practice was under-taken in pairs and groups; the emphasis was shifted away from public question and answer sessions. Most teachers observe that as boys grow older they grow more reluctant to answer questions in class by putting up their hands. This can be attributed to peer pressure which interprets any public demonstration of co-operation with the teacher as a threat to their image and status in the group. This is something to which teachers need to be sensitive.

There is a strong argument for incorporating more pair- and groupwork with boys and girls to boost their confidence.

Pairwork exercises do not have to be prolonged and can usefully be implemented at the beginning of the lesson as a means of attuning pupils to the foreign language again. Some examples of warm-up pairwork activities are given below. They can be used to revise sequences of words, such as days of the week, months, numbers or the alphabet; with word fields such as colours, adjectives or hobbies; or as a means of revising vocabulary covered in the previous lesson.

- Word tennis: pupils 'bat' words backwards and forwards to each other, miming a game of table tennis.

- One pupil takes on the role of the teacher and instructs their partner how to say words, for instance, slowly, quickly, quietly, loudly.

- One pupil traces a number or word on the back of their partner, and their partner has to say the word or number out loud.

- Lip-reading: one pupil mouths a word, and the other has to say it out loud.

- One pupil mimes or draws a word, e.g. hobbies, and the other guesses.

- Brainstorm 10 words that came up in the previous lesson as quickly as possible. The first pair to complete put up their hands and are then asked to demonstrate to the rest of the class.

- Completing an ID form. This idea comes from John Hill at the University of Nottingham and works particularly well as an ice-breaker at the beginning of a term. The form below is intended for use with higher ability pupils, or sixth-form students, but it can be adapted in order to reduce the amount of language that the pupils need. The pupils are each given two copies of the ID form below, with the phrases printed in the target language:

ID Form

First name:

Surname:

Age:

Date of birth:

Marital status:

Brothers & sisters:

Hobbies:

Favourite colour:

Favourite food:

Favourite TV programme:

Hero/heroine:

Holiday destination last year:

Ambition:

The teacher explains that the pupils must ask her/him the relevant questions so that they can fill in the teacher's ID form. This provides an excellent opportunity to revise the question forms that the pupils will need in the next stage. The pupils are usually highly motivated to ask the questions as they are eager to uncover the teacher's deepest secrets. The teacher's answers, which can be written up on the board or OHP, provide the pupils with a written model. The form can also integrate a small box in the right-hand corner where pupils are invited to sketch the teacher. Comparing their sketches provides a great source of amusement.

Pupils are then instructed to fill in the form for a partner; this involves them taking it in turns to ask each other the questions. (It is simpler if one form is completed before starting on the second.) It is useful to have some dictionaries around the room so that pupils can look up unknown vocabulary.

When all forms have been completed, the teacher asks each person to select the three most interesting facts about their partner and report them to the rest of the class. Again, pupils usually find it interesting to discover something new about their classmates and this presents the teacher with a valuable opportunity to brush up the pupils' use of the possessive pronouns, 'her' and 'his'.

Pairwork can clearly only be carried out with classes over which the teacher feels that they have good control, but such warm-up activities are likely to make pupils feel more confident about contributing in front of the whole class. Increased pairwork opportunities may help to overcome the problem of girls' reticence. The following hints may help you to structure pairwork effectively:

Golden rules for successful pairwork

- Ensure that pupils are equipped with all the language that they will need for the pairwork activity, including the questions that they will ask.

- Ensure that pupils are confident with the pronunciation of language, particularly of questions. This may involve some choral repetition before the pairwork commences.

- Give clear instructions. If these are in the target language ask one pupil to interpret for the others, or ask one competent pair to model the exercise for others.

- Set a time limit and let the pupils know what this is.

- Signal gestures/phrases needed for beginning and ending pairwork. This could be a thumbs up/thumbs down gesture. Putting up your hand, and having the pupils imitate you as soon as they see you, is a technique that is frequently used in drama lessons and can be very effective for bringing pairwork to a close.

- Feedback – consider its necessity and function. Is it always necessary? If you want the pairwork to be a piece of summative assessment you might want to hear a couple of pairs perform their role-play, or demonstrate their pairwork exercise, so that you can record a grade or comment in your markbook. If the purpose is formative assessment, however, you might simply want to listen out for common errors or misunderstandings and then cover these with the class as a whole when the pairwork has finished.

Confidence-building exercises v accuracy

One risk of such pairwork exercises is that pupils pronounce words inaccurately. However, such independent learning tasks do leave the language teacher to wander around the classroom, listening out for common mispronunciations, and then work on these with the whole class.

There are certain dangers in correcting individuals' pronunciation in front of the class since many pupils' confidence is seriously affected by such public error correction. This raises the question of whether we focus on accuracy at the cost of confidence. Again, the Cleveland teachers decided that they would relax their insistence on spoken accuracy, and reported that another of the results of their pilot was that boys developed better accents. Below are some ideas on how we might approach error correction in order to avoid embarrassing pupils:

Dos and Don'ts of error correction

Do give pupils who are struggling to give you an answer a choice of words, e.g.
Teacher: Hast du Haustiere, Becky? (Have you got any pets, Becky?)
Pupil: Ich … (I…)
Teacher: Eine Katze? Einen Hund? (A cat? A dog?)
Pupil: Ich habe eine Katze.

Do model the correct answer, e.g.
Teacher: Qu'est-ce que tu as fait le weekend, Harry? (What did you do at the weekend, Harry?)

Pupil: [*is unable to answer*]
Teacher: Moi, je suis allée au cinéma (I went to the cinema).
Pupil: Je suis allé au cinéma.

Do Answer the question yourself – with an example, e.g.:
Teacher: Ou habites-tu, David? (Where do you live, David?)
Pupil: Je m'appelle David. (I'm called David)
Teacher: Oui, tu t'appelles David et tu habites Solihull ou Leeds ou Birmingham? (Yes, you're called David and do you live in Solihull or Leeds or Birmingham?)

Do ensure that you give pupils adequate time to reflect on and answer your question. This is obviously very difficult when you are trying to retain the attention of 29 other children, but research has proven that the 'waiting time' allowed by the teacher before the pupil responds significantly affects children's progress and confidence. It might be worth inviting one of your colleagues to observe you teaching, making this a specific focus for their observation. They could time how long you wait before intervening and inform you whether they thought that this was long enough.

Do repeat a pupil's inaccurate answer, amending it to make it correct, e.g.
Pupil: Je ne regarde jamais la télé la weekend.
Teacher: Très intéressant, tu ne regardes jamais la télé *le* weekend.

Do respond to an error by asking the whole class to repeat the correct answer. This distances the child from the error and means that they are no longer the sole focus of your attention, e.g.
Pupil: Ich wohnt in einem Doppelhaus.
Teacher to whole class: Alle zusammen. Ich wohne in einem Doppelhaus.

Do come back to the question, if you can, later in the lesson. This gives the pupil a second chance to produce the correct answer and helps them to re-wire the responsible neural networks!

Do praise the correct part of an answer (if there is one), reassuringly pointing out the error, e.g.
Teacher: Tu as des frères ou des soeurs, Michael? (Have you got any brothers or sisters, Michael?

Pupil: Tu as un frère. (You have a brother).
Teacher: Bon, Michael. Presque parfait. *J'ai* (pointing to oneself) un frère. (Good, Michael. Nearly perfect. *I've* got a brother).

Don't simply dismiss an incorrect answer with a 'Non', 'Nein', shake of the head or by moving on to someone else with no acknowledgement at all.

Don't repeat the question at increasing volume!

Pupils can, of course, only become confident speakers if the teacher sequences tasks so that support is withdrawn gradually until pupils are able to produce the language independently. The following diagram maps out one possible way of doing this:

The development of speaking skills

Repetition/drilling/imitation
↓
Teacher support is gradually reduced
(guessing games/teacher gives pupils two options to choose from)
↓
Structured pairwork
(pupils have access to visuals or textual prompts as a framework)
↓
Teacher-led questions and answers
↓
Pupils give opinions, ask questions, deal with the unpredictable

In order to enable pupils to speak the language independently it is most important to remember that the lesson must first concentrate primarily on receptive skills (listening, reading) before turning to productive skills (speaking, writing).

Making speaking a means to an end

While girls have fewer inhibitions about opening up and discussing feelings, and their personal lives, and chatting, boys' talk tends to be functional and objective. If, by the age of 15/16, this reticence and lack of personal curiosity is combined with the insecurity of adolescence, it does not look too good for the GCSE oral, when the 'Personal Identification' questions are being repeated for the umpteenth time. Boys do not generally respond well to being asked what the weather is like in the summer, to describe their hamsters or the teacher sitting in front of them, or, in the worst possible case to being asked 'Darren, comment t'appelles-tu?' This is speaking for its own sake; boys are not interested in it because they can't perceive the point.

Communicative language teaching has provided us with something of a solution. It allows for meaningful communication, where the aim is to fill in the information gap. A good example of how boys respond to tasks where speaking has these two different functions was observed in a class of Year 8 boys. The class was working on describing people in French. When the teacher asked one boy to describe himself to the rest of the class the other boys were inattentive. When a second boy was then asked to describe someone else, while the others guessed who was being described, the class were immediately engaged. This is an obvious demonstration of communicative language teaching principles, but reinforces the point that boys will respond more positively if the speaking task has an information gap.

Pairwork activities can easily be devised that have an information gap. Here are a few examples:

- *Directions*: each pupil has a map of a town with various buildings shown on it. At the bottom of their sheet are pictures of buildings that they must locate on their map. Their partner gives them directions so that they can mark the buildings on their map. The two maps are then compared to verify whether the directions were correctly followed.

- *Describing rooms*: each pupil has a picture of a room with various pieces of furniture in it. There are some differences between the pictures, however, and the pupils must spot these differences by asking each other questions, such as 'Where is the guitar?', 'Is there a bookcase in the room?' etc.

- *Happy Families*. I bought this game at a table-top sale for ten pence and it proved to be such a popular teaching resource that I wished I could have bought a truck-load. In the absence of the commercially manufactured game, give each pupil a sheet of pictures of faces or pictures of people. The faces should be numbered, lettered or have names. Pupil A describes a face or person to Pupil B who must guess the correct number, letter or name. Pupil A gives them one sentence only to begin with, such as 'Il a des cheveux noirs', after which Pupil B makes a guess. If the guess is correct, Pupil B takes over, if not Pupil A gives them another clue and so on. The aim is for Pupil B to guess the identity of the person as quickly as possible.

Mobility

Mobility is often cited as an important variable in enhancing boys' learning; owing to their socialization boys often learn through doing rather than through being passive listeners. And girls also respond enthusiastically to activities which get them out of their chairs. *'Moving around the classroom, interviewing others'* proved to be one of the most popular tasks included in questionnaires. But boys often recognize themselves that such activities require a certain amount of self-discipline that is sometimes lacking among boys, as boys in Year 8 recognized:

AB: How about this one, 'Moving around the classroom, interviewing others?'
Boy 1: We ain't done that.
AB: But if you were to do it?
Boy 1: Chaos.
Boy 2: It would be funny, 'cos we'd all be messing about.
Boy 3: Everybody would be running around.

Getting pupils to arrange themselves in a row according to a particular sequence is a good way of encouraging them to use questions and answers. For instance, pupils are instructed to put themselves in order of age, with the youngest at one end of the room and the oldest at the other end. This involves them having to ask and answer the question: 'When is your birthday?' Another sequence can involve the number of their house, with the lowest number at one end of the room, and placing themselves in alphabetical order according to their surname. This latter exercise is excellent if pupils need extra practice in using a dictionary.

Other ideas for surveys are:

- Proverbs. These are written out on cards, with the beginning of a proverb on one card and the ending on another. Pupils have to find the person who has the part that matches their beginning or ending. This gives older, higher ability pupils and sixth-form students a fascinating insight into the culture of the language.

- Find someone who... Pupils seek the person who matches the criteria set by the teacher. These could include:

  - goes to bed at 11 o'clock
  - goes to bed the latest
  - has a dog
  - has the most pets
  - has a birthday in December
  - likes swimming
  - whose telephone number has a 4 in it
  - who has met a famous person
  - who has been to France the most often

- The following survey can be used to set pupils up in pairs. Pupils complete the grid below, ticking the appropriate box when they find someone who has the same favourites as them. The person who has the greatest number of ticks next to their name at the end of the exercise becomes their partner.

Écrivez en français/allemand/espagnol le nom de:

  - ta boisson préfèrée: _____
  - ta couleur préfèrée _____
  - ton passetemps préfèré _____

TROUVEZ MAINTENANT LA PERSONNE QUI A LES MÊME RÉPONSES!

NOM	BOISSON (✓ OU X)	PASSETEMPS (✓ OU X)	COULEUR (✓ OU X)

Creativity

It is hard enough to persuade many boys to speak at length on any topic; they are even less likely to do so on a topic in which they have no interest and perceive as pointless. There is, therefore, an argument for giving pupils more creative scope, as they have in English lessons, to talk and write about their own interests. The addition of the 'Presentation' to examination boards' specifications for the GCSE speaking test has offered teachers an ideal opportunity to give pupils some free rein and talk about something in which they are genuinely interested. English teachers frequently report how successfully 'presentation' lessons engage pupils, when they are invited to talk about their interests and arrive at school equipped with tractors, aquarium equipment and a variety of small animals!

However, the fear among many MFL teachers is that pupils will not have the necessary vocabulary to articulate their interests, and consequently will be unable to say anything at all. Having examined a large number of presentations, and been paid for listening to the silence that ensues when the teacher prompts the pupil to talk about their family in the presentation section of the exam, I would argue that it is far better to have pupils saying a few words on a topic that is of personal interest to them than to have them say nothing at all on a topic chosen by the teacher.

If pupils are going to be able to express themselves in the target language, they will need to become independent learners who are able to access unknown vocabulary by themselves, in a glossary or dictionary. It is important that we teach pupils how to access such resources, even though dictionaries can no longer be used in the GCSE Examination. Chapter 4, Reading, looks at strategies for teaching pupils how to use dictionaries.

Pupils, particularly boys, are also far more likely to say more if they adopt a new identity. It is much more stimulating, and much less threatening, for boys to describe to a partner what they, as David Beckham, did the previous evening or weekend, rather than describe what they themselves did. Their partner is also motivated to listen since they have an information gap to fill in guessing the identity of their partner. Boys also need to be encouraged to indulge in such creativity in the speaking test if they are to cope with questions that they would not normally answer at length in their first language.

Expressing opinions

If pupils are to secure higher grades at GCSE level they need to be able to express their opinions. Having a range of opinion words at their disposal also enables the pupils to use language more spontaneously and independently. Having equipped the pupils with a range of simple opinion words you ask for their views on a range of items that are bound to provoke a response. These could include:

What do you think of ...
... David Beckham?
... school uniform?
... Eminem?
... Harry Potter?

To encourage older, higher ability pupils and sixth-form students to be less reticent explain to them that there is an invisible line along the middle of the classroom floor. At one end of this line you place a large card with 'I don't agree at all' in the target language on it, and at the other end a card displaying 'I fully agree'. You provide the students with a number of controversial statements and ask them to stand at a point on the line that best represents their opinion. Students are then asked to justify their position. Controversial statements could include:

- A woman should give up work when she has children.

- The use of cannabis should be made legal.

- Pupils should be allowed to leave school at 14.

Drama

Numerous boys in research interviews described their enjoyment of drama, compared with only a handful of more self-confident girls. MFL teachers frequently agree that boys enjoy drama in lessons because they feel more confident hiding behind a clear-cut imaginary role rather than struggling to be themselves in class. It is far easier, and more acceptable, for boys to talk about shopping or holidays when they are wearing a funny hat or are allowed to adopt a funny voice.

MFL and drama clearly have a lot in common; both require pupils to suspend their disbelief. When pupils enter the MFL classroom we are asking them to pretend that they are in a foreign environment where the main language of communication is a foreign language. This, together with the reason given above, is a strong case for maximizing our use of drama in MFL.

We should not forget that performing in front of a whole group is an intimidating experience for many pupils, and adults. If one of the purposes of using drama is to make pupils feel more confident about using the foreign language, we need to ensure that they feel secure. Below are a number of drama activities which do not involve changing the layout of the classroom, may only take five minutes, and that do not necessarily involve performing in front of the group:

- Pupils work in pairs. One pupil reads out their account of a holiday, or any other text. Their partner tells them how to read it, using a range of adverbs in the target language –

slowly, quickly, angrily, sadly, excitedly. This activity can either practise simple adverbs with Key Stage 3 pupils or more complex adverbs with AS students, such as cautiously, wearily or seductively!

- A variation of the same task involves pupils producing a pile of cards with adverbs written on them. A volunteer mimes an activity that is chosen by the rest of the class, such as opening a door, having a wash, knitting, or walking the dog, demonstrating that adverb. The rest of the class have to guess the adverb.

- The following activity was suggested by Helen Aberdeen, an MFL Teacher at Sir Bernard Lovell Language College in Bristol. She has been working together with the drama department to make MFL lessons more motivating. The pupils stand in a circle. The first person steps forward into the circle and says their first name. As they say it they accompany it with a gesture that says something about them. As soon as they have completed the gesture, everyone else in the circle steps forward and repeats their name and gesture. The activity proceeds in a clockwise direction and pupils are reassured that it does not matter if the gesture has already been done. This activity can be used as a lesson starter, to boost pupils' confidence. Standing in a circle reduces individuals' status and makes the pupils more dependent on each other for support. It can be adapted to practise specific MFL points in the following ways:

  - pupils say the names of buildings, accompanied by gestures. This aids memorization for pupils with kinaes-thetic learning styles, many of whom are boys. A railway station, for instance, would have someone moving their arms like a train, and a church would have someone with both hands clasped together as if in prayer
  - in the same way, pupils practise leisure activities
  - assisted by the teacher, pupils rehearse words that are difficult to pronounce, or are asked to say their favourite words. Gestures should, as far as possible, match the way the word is said

- Pupils often feel embarrassed about the foreign noises they are expected to make, so a loosening up exercise can help them to feel less embarrassed. In pairs, only one person is allowed to use 'yes', the other person 'no'. The 'yes' person must try to convince the 'no' person to agree. This exercise also focuses pupils' attention on intonation, an important part of pronunciation, and on those important little words that are all too easily forgotten in the GCSE examination. 'Please' can be substituted for 'yes'.

- Pupils are often turned off by the words 'role-play' and role-play is often associated with repeating transactional phrases off by heart. 'Improvisation', or 'impro' might be a more engaging term and pupils are likely to be more motivated if they are allowed to ham up the role-play. Invite them to act out a dialogue in different movie styles: horror movie; love story; Western; science fiction film; costume drama; musical!

- The following shopping role-play exercise is useful for bringing together all the shopping vocabulary and giving pupils the opportunity to use the language with a degree of spontaneity. It helps to prepare them for the unpredictable element of the GCSE role-play. Pupils first write out a shopping list, having been instructed that they must buy fruit or vegetables, meat, something from the bakery, something from the chemist and another grocery item. They must include the number or weight of the items, e.g. 200g cheese or three bread rolls. Five shopkeepers are then nominated and sit behind desks representing the various shops. They each have a card in front of them on the desk that displays the name of the shop. On the back of the card is their script, for instance 'Good morning', 'What would you like?', 'Would you like a bag?', 'Is that all?' The scripts must vary from card to card so that the customers have to listen very carefully to the shopkeeper in order to respond appropriately. The customers then set about acquiring their shopping list items by visiting all of the shops. A time limit is given by the teacher and once this is reached the activity re-starts with new shopkeepers. The role-play can be set in other contexts, such as in a restaurant. In this case the class is divided into pairs or threes, with one person playing the waiter and one or two playing the customer(s). The waiters are given scripts which have slight variations.

- Miming activities in pairs (one pupil mimes, the other guesses): animals; numbers, or letters of the alphabet with younger classes; hobbies; verbs in the past tense with older children.

- This is a good way of practising everyday routine phrases such as 'I wash my hair', 'I have my breakfast', ' I walk to school', and 'I clean my teeth'. It certainly enlivens this rather dull topic! The exercise is adapted from the TV improvisation programme, 'Whose Line is it, Anyway?', which has lots of drama ideas that could be adapted for use in the classroom. One pupil stands behind another. The pupil in front puts their arms behind their back and the person behind them slots their own arms through their partner's arms. The person behind must then use their arms to mime everyday routine activities, which the class guesses. The teacher could give the phrases written on cards to the pupil behind; this might speed the activity up a little. The cards might have been prepared by the class beforehand. It is easier to mime the activities if the pair are of a similar height, although the fun generated by having two differently sized people should not be missed! It is also sensible to pair up pupils of the same sex.

- The following role-play exercise does not have to involve drama at all. It is a conventional translation-based exercise that higher-ability pupils find particularly useful to help them memorize role-play phrases. The top half of an A4 sheet has a dialogue in the target language (TL). The bottom half has a translation of this and there is a horizontal line dividing the two. Having heard the role-play being modelled, either on tape or by the teacher, the pupils read it aloud in pairs. The English translation gives them access to the meaning of the text. When they feel sufficiently confident they fold the sheet in half along the horizontal line. They read out the dialogue in the TL, with the English version only in front of them. If they get stuck they can flip over to consult the TL version. After some practice the teacher can recall the pupils and ask them to feed back as a whole class. The teacher selects one pupil to read out the first line, consulting the English text only. This pupil then selects the next victim and so on, until the whole dialogue has been read out in the TL.

Games

Boys, and girls, love games and often comment on their disappearance from lessons in Key Stage 4. For some boys, games are the only redeeming feature of language lessons. When I asked one boy to rank French alongside other school subjects, with his favourite at the top and his least favourite at the bottom, his response was as follows:

It's nearly at the bottom for me ... just that far [thumb and finger a centimetre apart] from the bottom. That little bit at the bottom is just for the games.

In my questionnaire survey of pupils, 'Playing games with flashcards' was extremely popular with both sexes, but there is a particularly strong argument for providing boys with the visual props offered by flashcards. Girls generally have fewer problems remembering words; the visual or tactile element, it seems, is perhaps more important for boys who find memorizing words more difficult. We forget too easily that our first language is usually acquired through being bombarded with visual images; young children's books are replete with illustrations. It could be argued that we withdraw the visual support too early for many visual learners. Below are a few suggestions for flashcard games.

- on the teacher's command, pupils repeat individual words loudly and quietly, i.e. the teacher shows a picture of a train station, says 'Laut' and pupils shout 'Der Bahnhof'
- similarly, pupils repeat words slowly and quickly

- the teacher asks only girls or only boys to repeat, or one side of the classroom then the other

- the teacher asks only people with brown hair/blue eyes/ names beginning with 'A' to repeat

- the teacher displays all flashcards, then removes one and asks which one is missing

- the teacher reveals one card very slowly

- the teacher 'flashes' the card to the class

- the teacher shows the whole pack of flashcards to the group and asks pupils to remember which order they were shown in

- the teacher hands out flashcards to individuals in the class and instructs them to turn them over. The rest of the class have to remember either who has the card with 'Der Bahnhof' on it (for lower ability pupils, or as a receptive activity to be used early on in the flashcard sequence) or to name the flashcard that an individual is holding (for higher ability pupils, or as a productive activity to be used when pupils are confident in their knowledge of words)

- Mexican wave: the teacher divides the class into 3 or 4 groups from left to right and each group repeats part of a longer phrase, i.e. Je voudrais (first group repeats while standing up and throwing up their arms) des (second group) pommes frites (third group)

- lip-reading: the teacher picks a flashcard and silently mouths the word. Pupils guess what is on the flashcard.

Packaging simple activities as challenging games has an equally motivating effect on boys at Key Stage 4. One such example was observed in a Year 10 boys' group during the last lesson on a Tuesday. The teacher, Nick Jones, announced that the class was about to practise the irregular verbs, pouvoir, vouloir and devoir. He then asked the boys how long it would take for each of them to stand up, say part of the conjugated verb (i.e. je dois, tu dois, il doit, etc.) and sit down again. He then timed their performance against their estimate.

This episode was particularly interesting not only because it transformed a relatively mundane exercise into something challenging for the boys, but also because it resulted in the boys exerting positive peer pressure on Dwayne, slumped lifelessly over his desk at the outset, to participate. Within a few minutes he was as involved as the rest, desperate to prove himself to the teacher. Challenges of this kind, involving the pupils estimating how quickly they can do something and then setting out to prove themselves to the teacher, are very effective in motivating boys. A further example of this kind is 'Chinese whispers', where pupils in two teams race against each other to pass on a message in the target language to their neighbour.

Games that have a competitive element are highly likely to appeal to boys, particularly if boys are competing against the girls or pupils against the teacher, prof. v plebs! It is important, however, that the teams are not always male v female. Boys can take competitive games very seriously so this may engender hostility towards the girls. Some competitive games are described below:

- Vokabelnvolleyball (vocabulary volleyball). This is a good game for revising vocabulary at the end of a unit or at the end of a lesson. Pupils are divided into two teams. The teams are given 5 minutes to brainstorm vocabulary that they have just learned. When the 5 minutes are up they stand in two lines facing each other and each pupil is given a number that they are asked to remember (1–10 if there are 20 in the class). The teacher calls out a number and the pupil from each team with the corresponding number must call out a word that has just been learned. The two pupils are not allowed to confer with their team-mates, or to repeat the word that the other pupil said. This continues until a pupil is unable to provide a word; no repetition is allowed.

- The teacher draws a line down the middle of the board and writes numbers in digits that pupils have just learned. The class is divided into two teams and pupils numbered off. When the teacher calls out a number the two pupils with those numbers walk up to the blackboard and wait for the teacher to call out a number on the board. The pupils then either erase the corresponding digit on their side of the board or circle it. The first pupil to erase or circle the correct number wins a point for their team. This game can be played with a whole range of vocabulary, and flashcards can be stuck onto the board in place of words. To speed the game up the teacher can call out the number/word to be erased or circled first, then call out the pupils' numbers.

- Twenty envelopes are pasted onto a large sheet of card that is displayed on the classroom wall. A number, 1–20, is written on the front of each envelope in large script. The teacher places into the envelopes twenty small cards, ten with pictures, the other ten showing the corresponding words. The object of the game is for teams to match up the words with the pictures. Each team in turn calls out two numbers and the teacher shows the whole class the cards contained in those envelopes. If the cards match, the teacher removes them and awards the team one point. If they do not match the teacher replaces the cards and moves on to the next team. Pupils are not allowed to write anything down. If the teacher is feeling generous the numbers of removed cards can be written up on the board; if not, the pupils have to remember which envelopes are empty. The game can be played with all abilities, including sixth-formers, if the envelope contents are changed accordingly. An English translation of the matching target language word can replace a picture, and verbs in the present and past tense can be matched. The game is immensely popular with pupils and, if you have your own classroom, the poster can be left permanently on the wall to be used in spare moments or as a reward for pupils.

- TV quiz shows such as 'Who wants to be a Millionaire?', 'The Weakest Link' and 'Mastermind' can be easily adapted for use in the classroom. Using Powerpoint to present the questions and answers can add to the suspense, make them even more appealing and allow them to be re-used.

- Twenty questions: this is an effective means of getting the pupils to practise question forms that are all too often forgotten in the GCSE speaking exam. The teacher conceals a card that has a picture of a celebrity on it and the pupils must guess the celebrity's identity. Only questions that can be answered with yes or no may be asked. If the pupils fail to guess the celebrity in twenty questions they lose the game. If they succeed, the pupil who made the winning guess takes on the role of the teacher.

Problems and solutions

The following table summarizes some of the problems that pupils encounter when trying to speak a foreign language, and can be used to find possible strategies that take them into account. The second table includes some possible solutions.

Factors which may inhibit pupils' willingness to speak the FL:
Problems and solutions

Problem:
Motivation lacking in using FL to re-name concepts already labelled in mother tongue

Solution:

Problem:
The artificial environment of the MFL classroom

Solution:

Problem:
Embarrassment

Solution:

Problem:
Lack of real purpose in using spoken language

Solution:

Factors which may inhibit pupils' willingness to speak the FL:
Problems and possible solutions

Problem:
Motivation lacking in using FL to re-name concepts already labelled in mother tongue

Solution:
Make language learning exciting – through creativity and using FL for real communication.

Problem:
The artificial environment of the MFL classroom

Solution:
Re-create a mini France/Germany/Spain/Italy/Russia through immersion in the TL. Use other voices: FLA; video; tape; colleague.

Problem:
Embarrassment

Solution:
Pair- and group-work
Careful error correction

Problem:
Lack of real purpose in using spoken language

Solution:
Information gap
Give pupils FL phrases equivalent to those they would use in their first language

3 Listening

The difficulty of listening

Listening is often perceived by students, from Key Stage 3 pupils to undergraduate students, as the most difficult skill to master, as pupils frequently reported in interviews:

> *Year 8 boys*
> S: The problem with the listening tapes is because they're, like, French, and it's fluent. It's really hard to understand them because, like, Miss X, she can understand what they're saying but I can't understand them. . .
> C: Same with us. Miss, teacher, will say it differently to what's on the tape.

Both boys and girls in interviews frequently commented that they found the transition from listening to the teacher's carefully paced and familiar voice to listening to a strange, faceless, fast recorded voice very difficult. What pupils reportedly find most problematic about listening is the pace of recorded material.

It is worth remembering that MFL makes more demands on pupils' aural skills than any other subject. This makes it a particularly challenging subject for boys whose aural skills are often inferior to girls'; research on interactional styles has found that boys are not good at listening to others. In MFL we are, therefore, asking boys to do something that they don't do especially well in their first language.

Boys' inferior listening skills present MFL teachers with significant problems, as many teachers reported.

> . . . you can tell them till you're blue in the face what you want them to do. I perhaps shouldn't say this, but I have to speak to them a lot more in English than I do to the girls, because it

doesn't go in if you speak to them in French. They're not listening really. They switch off.

(Year 7 mixed ability boys' teacher)

Listening is also often regarded by pupils as a passive process. This perception may conflict with pupils' preferred learning styles if, as is often the case with boys, their socialization has encouraged them to learn through doing.

Making listening purposeful

The listening task format clearly influences boys' generally negative attitude to listening. While boys are often not good at listening for its own sake, they respond well to communicative listening exercises which require them to fill in an information gap.

A typically passive task, 'listening to a foreign language assistant talking about school or Christmas in their home country', ranked in my research among those activities least enjoyed by boys. This contrasted with their much more enthusiastic response to the prospect of the more active variation, 'asking a foreign language assistant questions'.

Video can play an important role in motivating boys to listen; boys were generally much more motivated than girls by the prospect of using videos in lessons. Both sexes can gain a lot from video when it is used in a highly structured way. Purposeful, structured viewing is necessary if girls are to overcome their anxiety at not being able to understand everything on the video, and boys are to resist the temptation of putting their feet up. It should be remembered that video is very often extremely difficult to access for pupils. Therefore it may be worth preparing pupils for what they are about to watch by asking them to predict the sorts of words they might hear in the recording or to clarify any difficult language points that may arise. Below are a few ideas of how video can be used to make purposeful listening exercises:

- the video is paused and pupils and asked to predict what happens next. Depending on their ability, they could write the script and act it out, mime the next scene or do a 'living statues' tableau, draw a picture or describe in narrative form what happens next.

- pupils listen to the dialogue only (the TV can be turned around) and describe what's happening on the video, or produce a storyboard

- pupils produce the English subtitles for a short video clip

- pupils complete a grid with information such as how often, what order, who says what. . .

- pupils decide whether statements describing the video clip are true or false and higher ability pupils correct the incorrect statements

- pupils are given a word or phrase and put their hands up, or stand up, each time they hear it. This helps to train pupils to listen for detail. Alternatively, pupils are given a topic area and have to signal when this is mentioned on the video.

Further ideas for listening activities which have an information gap, and encourage pupils to listen to each other, are as follows:

- *Cops & Robbers.* This is a more enjoyable alternative to the conventional survey task that pupils undertake towards the beginning of a language course in order to practise saying their name, where they live and how old they are. Half the class is given blue cards to indicate that they are the cops. The other half is given red cards to indicate that they are the robbers. Each card contains information in the target language in the following format:

FIRST NAME:
SURNAME:
AGE:
PLACE OF RESIDENCE:

The information on the cops' cards is a profile of the suspect; that on the robbers' cards is information about them as the robber. The object of the game is for the cops to catch their robber by finding the person with the matching card. To make the game more difficult, and last longer, it is important to include very similar information on the cards so that pupils have to ask all of the questions. There might, therefore, be 12 Wolfgang Schmidts in the class who are all

32 years old but there is only one who lives in Hannover. Pupils need to be instructed that they will have to practise their alphabet as the cops will ask them how to spell their name. When the robbers have been caught the cops can take them into custody in one corner of the classroom.

- *'Spot the lie'*. This game was devised by Paul Wyton, formerly Head of Department at Copley High School. It provides an excellent means of motivating pupils to listen to each other and to use all four core skills. It should be used towards the end of a unit working on holidays. The whole class is presented with a short text describing the teacher's recent holiday and spend some time working through this. The text consists of simple sentences like 'Last summer I went to France. I travelled by plane. I spent two weeks there and stayed in a hotel.' The teacher then removes the text and shows the class a series of symbols that graphically represent it. 'France', for instance, is depicted by a French flag and 'plane' by a picture of a plane. The teacher reads out the text again, but this time adds a further detail not represented in the pictures, or makes a deliberate mistake. It is the pupils' task to 'spot the lie'. The class works through a couple of further examples provided by the teacher. They are then given a piece of card and instructed to write a text, based on the teacher's model, on one side and a series of pictures on the other. There must be a discrepancy between the pictures and the text; for instance a ship could be included in the pictures while the text includes the word 'plane'. The pupils then work in pairs, holding up their card so that their partner can see the pictures only. They read out the text in full and when they have finished their partner has to spot the deliberate mistake.

- *Dominoes*. Half the class is issued with a card with a question in the target language on it, the other half have a card with an answer. The questions are numbered. The person with Question 1 reads it out to the whole class, and the person with the corresponding answer must read it out. The person with Question 2 continues until everyone in the class has contributed. This can also be done with opposites – black, white; small, large etc. – or with verbs in different tenses, e.g. present and perfect; present and future. To ensure that pupils are still listening after they have read out their card they are informed that merits will be awarded to pupils who are able to answer questions put by the teacher about the content of the cards at the end of the exercise.

- *Listening to other pupils performing role-plays.* While pupils are generally happy to listen to the first pair of pupils performing their dialogue after a pairwork session, they are likely to turn off after this unless they have an activity to complete. It is a good idea to use this opportunity to encourage pupils to express their opinions of what they have just heard, e.g. 'super!'; 'affreux'; 'ausgezeichnet'; 'nicht schlecht'. Opinion words are all-important in the GCSE exam and frequent use of them in this way will ensure that pupils have lots of practice. It is also important that pupils are given translations of these target language opinion words that are derived from the most recent bank of opinion words in English. At the moment these words include 'random' and 'vivid'. This should help to make them more relevant and exciting to pupils. Pupils can also be asked to grade the performance on a scale of one to ten, and justify their grade either in English or the target language; be asked to comment in English on the role-play using the GCSE speaking test assessment criteria; or else answer questions about the content of the role-play.

- *Taking the register at the beginning of the lesson.* This routine can be expanded to make it into part of the learning rather than merely an administrative routine. Pupils are asked to give a word in the target language when their name is called; this could be a word from the previous lesson, or else part of a sequence such as the alphabet, numbers or months. Pupils are encouraged to listen to each other by the teacher asking a question about the pupils' responses at the end of the register, e.g. 'Who said. . .?' or 'What did Charlotte say?'

'Hands-on' listening tasks

While boys are often not good passive listeners, activities which involve applying the information they have gained from listening are much more motivating to them. Boys in the survey were much more positive than girls in their responses to the following tasks: 'following directions from a tape to find a building on a map'; 'listening to a tape and filling in a grid'; and 'listening to a description of someone wanted by the police and drawing that person'. Other examples of motivating hands-on tasks are given below:

- *Running dictation.* Pupils work in pairs, one acting as the scribe and the other as the runner. It is the job of the runner to find texts that are stuck on various walls of the classroom, memorize as much information as possible and pass this on verbally to the scribe who must write it down as accurately as possible. The runner is not allowed to write anything down. This activity can be made into a competition with a prize or merit being given to the first pair to produce the most accurate text. When all pupils have finished their attention can be focused on their written errors by the teacher displaying the correct text on the OHP. This is more motivating if pupils are marking each others' work. A further challenge can be added to the task if pupils are asked to put all texts, or sentences, into the correct order once they have collected them all. It is useful to include clock times in the texts if you choose to do this; a description of a typical day is a useful text.

- *Drawing what they hear.* As part of the unit on describing people and clothes, one pupil is given a picture of a person cut out of a catalogue or magazine. They describe the person to the rest of the class while the others produce their own sketches. The pupil can be given written prompts on their picture to help them. The pupils' sketches are then compared with the original picture, and the best resemblance selected.

- *Giving written feedback on performed role-plays.* Instead of giving verbal feedback, pupils write down their comments or grades on a table distributed by the teacher. The table can be used to introduce pupils to a selection of opinion words and assessment criteria before they are later able to give their opinions independently.

Training listening skills

Given that boys' listening skills are generally not as well-developed as girls', there is a strong argument for spending some time training pupils' listening skills before we introduce pupils to more complex aural exercises. We often throw these unsophisticated listeners in at the deep end, asking them to listen to a mass of foreign sounds, make sense of them by deducing the meaning of unfamiliar words from the context, and then paraphrase these words in a sentence. When pupils begin learning a foreign language it is particularly important that we boost their confidence in listening skills, rather than merely using the standard pre-recorded listening comprehension as a means of assessing pupils' understanding.

The sections below outline strategies that can be used in order to train pupils' listening skills.

Simple tasks

Rather than being asked to listen out for whole phrases or sentences, or translate part of the text, pupils are simply asked to count the number of times they hear a particular sound or word, or to put their hand up each time they hear it. This focuses pupils closely on pronunciation, and it is worthwhile selecting sounds that are commonly found in the target language such as 'au' in German or 'u' as in 'tu' in French.

Pupils can also be allocated words in a text that the teacher reads aloud. Every time they hear their word they stand up, when they hear it a second time they sit down and so on.

Listening props

Rather than using materials that are completely unfamiliar to pupils it is worth using stories or articles that already have some meaning to them. Fairy stories can be used in this way, as can local events in school. One of the teachers I observed chose a recent scandalous event in the class – one of the boys being run over by an unidentified female driver in the playground! – as the basis of his listening text. In this way pupils can be coaxed into forgetting the anxiety that usually accompanies listening.

Pupils can also be given extra support if visuals are used to support listening materials. Some teachers are making use of storytelling in MFL and a number of story books are available for use in primary MFL classrooms that can easily be adapted for use with secondary classes. It may be worth consulting your primary colleagues, if a language is taught in your feeder primary schools, to find out about their good practice.

The transcript of the listening text, such as cartoons that are often found in textbooks, can also be a useful prop in the early stages. The pupils follow the text in their books while listening to the recording. When the teacher stops the tape they have to provide the next word. This sort of exercise focuses pupils' attention on the interrelationship between sounds and writing.

Showing the pupils photographs of one's own family is a good way of introducing pupils to family and friends vocabulary. Pupils are invariably fascinated by seeing photos of the teacher's parents, grandparents, uncles and aunts and pets. Having shown the photos, accompanied by the new vocabulary, e.g. 'Das ist meine Mutti' / 'Voici ma mère' , the teacher can ask the pupils questions to test their memories and elicit the new vocabulary, e.g. 'Wer ist das?' / C'est qui?' and 'Wie heisst sie?' / Comment s'appelle-t-elle?'

Gestures
Many boys find it difficult to distinguish between sounds, so using gestures to underline the sound changes, for instance to highlight the endings on verbs – ich heiss**e**, du heiss**t** – will help them, and other kinaesthetic learners, to hear and remember the sounds more easily.

Songs
Songs can also usefully motivate pupils, and many can be easily accompanied by gestures. Pupils' interest in songs can be particularly effectively engaged if the teacher can find foreign artists who sing chart hits in the target language; in Spanish these

might include Shakira and Enrique Iglesias, and in French Celine
Dion. The Classic Pathfinder *Inspiring Performance (Focus on drama
and song)* has an excellent selection of songs of this kind (see under
CILT in *Recommended reading* and *Useful addresses* at the end of the
book). In adolescence boys may be less interested in singing,
unless the tune is a 'cool' tune or unless they are in competition
with the girls. It is worth asking pupils what current hits they like,
and adding some foreign language lyrics to the latest hit. The
American army marching chant, often seen in Hollywood movies
as soldiers are marching during training, offers a good basic
rhythm. Very simple lyrics can be added, as in the following
example:

Je m'appelle Amanda Barton.
J'ai trente et quatre ans.
J'ai un chat et un chien.
J'habite en Angleterre.

This provides pupils with an excellent model that they can then
adapt themselves. I have seen some outstanding examples of boys'
creativity when they have been asked to write a song themselves.

It also helps if boys can see a male teacher willing to make a fool
of himself by singing.

Pre-listening activities
Pupils are given a listening exercise and asked to predict the
answers before they hear the tape. This is also good training in
examination strategies as it encourages the pupils to read through
the questions carefully and use them to help them find the answer.
Pupils write their predictions down before they hear the
recording, then write answers in a second column or on a
separate page when they actually hear the tape. The class is then
asked how many of their predictions were correct, and how they
arrived at the correct answer. This can be made into a fun
competition with pupils acting as clairvoyants.

Listening to each other
Research has shown that boys, unlike girls, are not always good at
turn-taking. Passing a sponge football around the room can be a
good way of training boys to listen to each other; they only speak

when they're holding the football. If this is being done in a mixed classroom it is important to tell the pupils that they must throw the ball to a member of the opposite sex, otherwise the ball passing is restricted to one sex only.

One of the teachers I worked with nominated a 'Behaviour Manager' in her Year 9 boys' group every couple of weeks. When a boy spoke out of turn, without putting his hand up, he was given a yellow card by the Behaviour Manager. If he did it again, he was given a red card and subsequently a penalty, such as tidying up the classroom at the end of the lesson. This strategy worked extremely well with a class that the teacher described initially as her 'diarrhoea' class, a label that appeared to be fully appropriate. Other teachers have also experienced success in using the strategy with older groups, even in Year 11, but have reported that girls do not respond as positively.

Focus on pronunciation
Focusing closely on pronunciation can help pupils to develop their listening skills. The following strategies can all be used to do this:

- pupils repeat words privately, either with their headphones on, or simply with their hands cupped over their ears. This can be done as part of the introduction of new vocabulary, interspersed with choral repetition, or to practise words that are particularly difficult to pronounce. Younger children particularly enjoy creating their own listening booth by cupping their ears with their hands.

- CD-Roms. A number of CD-Roms now focus specifically on pronunciation and allow the user to see a native speaker's lips moving as they enunciate words. Pupils can be encouraged to bring in their own mirrors to compare the movement of their own lips with those of the speaker or the teacher.

- raise awareness of intonation: pupils, in pairs, say words or phrases to express particular emotions, e.g. disappointment, excitement, anger, sadness

- sound discrimination exercises: pupils put up their hands or stand up when they hear the odd one out in sequences such as the following: vu vous vu vu; schön schon schon schon; mato mato mato mató mato

- reciting poetry/dialogues from memory

- pupils record or video their own dialogues and the rest of the class assess pronunciation

- draw attention to particular pronunciation patterns early on in your teaching. I normally present students with a list of common, and problematic, sounds, e.g. 'au', 'ie' and 'ei' in German, then ask them to work out how they are pronounced by identifying words already known to them that contain them. I then present them with a list of unknown words, or German surnames, and we apply these pronunciation rules in order to work out how they would be pronounced.

- tongue-twisters allow pupils to laugh about the difficulties of pronunciation as well as exposing them to sounds that are not found in their first language. Some examples of French and German tongue-twisters are given below. Further examples, including tongue-twisters in Spanish, can be found at *www.uebersetzung.at/twister/es.htm*. This website also gives translations into English on request.

FRANÇAIS:

Je suis ce que je suis et si je suis ce que je suis, qu'est-ce que je suis?

Santé n'est pas sans *t*, mais maladie est sans *t*.

Les chaussettes de l'archiduchesse sont-elles sèches? Archisèches!

Mon père est maire, mon frère est masseur.

Ces cerises sont si sûres qu'on ne sait pas si c'en sont.

Un dragon gradé dégrade un gradé dragon.

Tes laitues naissent-elles? Si tes laitues naissent, mes laitues naîtront.

DEUTSCH:

Klaras Klasse kitzelt Klemens kleines Kind.

Zwischen zwei spitzen Steinen saßen zwei zischende Schlangen.

Der Koch roch auch in der Nacht nach Knoblauch.

Zehn zahme Ziegen zogen zehn Zentner Ziegel zur Ziegelei.

Die Katze tritt die Treppe krumm. Krumm tritt die Katze die Treppe

Weiße Borsten bürsten besser als schwarze Borsten bürsten.

Der Leutnant von Leuten befahl seinen Leuten, nicht eher zu läuten als der Leutnant von Leuten seinen Leuten das Läuten befahl.

Werler Waschweiber waschen weiße Wäsche. Weiße Wäsche waschen Werler Waschweiber.

In Ulm, um Ulm und um Ulm herum.

Blaukraut bleibt Blaukraut und Brautkleid bleibt Brautkleid.

Der Potsdamer Postkutscher putzt den Potsdamer Postkutschkasten.

Giving pupils control

Given that pupils' main difficulty with listening is the speed of recordings, it is well worth making full use of a language laboratory or multi-media suite in order to allow pupils to have some control over the speed of the tape. This is particularly valuable in the early stages but is also good practice for the AS and A2 examinations where students are allowed to pause the tape themselves. If you do not have access to such facilities it may be worth inviting pupils to bring in their own Walkmans, or setting aside a part of the lesson when pupils go off in groups to use a small cluster of tape-recorders and headphones.

Tasks presented as a challenge

Boys, in particular, respond well when listening exercises are presented as a challenge. Boys will visibly react to the teacher's challenge – 'This is probably the most difficult listening exercise you will have ever done. Do you think you're up to it?' – and will set about trying to prove the teacher wrong.

Listening to the teacher

My observations in classrooms revealed that boys listen best when they are being taught by teachers who dominate their attention, leaving them with little opportunity to do anything but listen. Effective teachers match their pupils' unpredictability by modulating their voices and moving around the classroom. Gradually reducing the volume of your voice once you have the pupils' attention, so that it ends up as little more than a whisper, is a good way of ensuring that pupils have to make an effort to listen.

4 Reading

There appear to be significant differences in boys' and girls' attitudes to reading. Boys who responded to the questionnaires I distributed ranked it as the least enjoyable of the four attainment targets: only 8 per cent of the boys in the three all-boys classes I observed claimed to enjoy reading in an FL. There are perhaps three main reasons for this disparity:

- boys' view of reading as a feminine, impractical activity
- boys' negative responses to fiction, and their association of reading with fiction
- pupils' lack of awareness of how to approach reading foreign language texts

Strategies for overcoming these obstacles are outlined below.

Do boys read?

It would be all too easy to believe from the tabloid headlines that boys do not read at all. This is clearly not the case; while boys do not always enjoy reading the same materials as girls, especially fiction and literature, they do often prefer to read the following text types:

- factual materials such as manuals and reviews
- illustrated materials such as comics and cartoons
- electronic texts via email, software or on the Internet

Visuals, the format in which the text is presented, and what pupils are asked to do with the information they gain from reading, are all important factors in motivating boys to read.

The Internet

Reading a text from the Internet has considerably more appeal to many boys than reading out of a book, and the Internet offers a plethora of excellent reading materials. Below is a list of useful websites together with brief descriptions of what they offer. The list includes both sites that have worksheets which can be downloaded for use in class as well as sites that pupils can access online.

Useful websites

http://www.linguanet.org.uk (A 'virtual language centre' can be found at Lingu@NET, which lists 200 language websites)

http://www.bbc.co.uk/education/languages/ (Lots of resources for French, German, Spanish and Italian and for a range of levels. Includes 'Le Français cool: A Guide to French slang')

http://www.ALLO-languages.org.uk (ALL website. Offers links to websites that are particularly suitable for adolescents, including Harry Potter, French football, the Tour de France and Friends.)

http://www.studyspanish.com/ (Lots of useful links to newspapers, jokes, comics and cultural notes. There is even a page explaining how to dance the Macarena!)

http://www.reallyusefulfrench.co.uk (Bursting with resources including grammar practice pages, programs to help teachers create resources and GCSE writing paper practice. Link to the really useful German site.)

http://www.bonjourdefrance.com (Lots of interactive games which are graded, and links to games and recipes. All in French, so pupils will need guidance.)

http://bonjour.org.uk (Very accessible for younger learners. Also has German and Spanish sister sites.)

www.spellmaster.com (Very useful for creating your own games.)

For boys in particular it is extremely important that any Internet-based exercise is clearly structured. It may occasionally be appropriate to set pupils the task of searching the Internet for information, such as in the fact-finding exercise described in Chapter 1 in which pupils research a target-language country. It is important, however, that when such tasks are set in class the pupils have a strict deadline to complete the search. Otherwise the temptation of finding unrelated, though equally interesting, material may prove too great.

The worksheets below are an example of the way in which a structured exercise can be based on Internet-based texts. Similar worksheets, prepared by PGCE trainees, can be found on the ALL website at *www.ALLO-languages.org.uk*.

By Kathryn Hill and Nicholas Munn

Harry Potter

1. Cliquez sur:-
   http://www.ifrance.com/potter/harry.htm

2. Cliquez sur 'Cartes d'identité' et répondez aux questions suivantes:
   A. Quel âge a Harry?
   B. Quelle est la date de son anniversaire?
   C. Où habite-il?
   D. A-t-il des frères ou des soeurs?
   E. Comment s'appelle sa mere?
   F. Quels sont ses signes particuliers?
   G. Qui est son ennemi principal?
   H. Est-ce qu'il a des animaux?
   I. Qui sont ses meilleurs amis?

3. Maintenant, en utilisant le format sur le site, faites une carte d'identité pour vous.

Laura O'Neill

Le cinéma français

1 – Premier pas :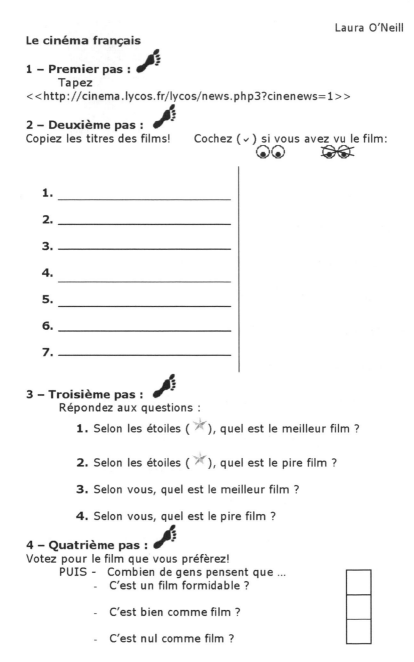
    Tapez
<<http://cinema.lycos.fr/lycos/news.php3?cinenews=1>>

2 – Deuxième pas :
Copiez les titres des films!   Cochez (✓) si vous avez vu le film:

    1. _____

    2. _____

    3. _____

    4. _____

    5. _____

    6. _____

    7. _____

3 – Troisième pas :
    Répondez aux questions :

        1. Selon les étoiles (✦), quel est le meilleur film ?

        2. Selon les étoiles (✦), quel est le pire film ?

        3. Selon vous, quel est le meilleur film ?

        4. Selon vous, quel est le pire film ?

4 – Quatrième pas :
Votez pour le film que vous préférez!
      PUIS -   Combien de gens pensent que ...
          -   C'est un film formidable ?

          -   C'est bien comme film ?

          -   C'est nul comme film ?

Making reading (inter)active

Having the opportunity to interact with the text, and do something with it, is of importance to boys. Hence, in my research, tasks such as 'reading about the different way of life in France', which have no practical outcome, predictably appealed less to boys than girls. Boys respond much more positively to reading when it is linked with the other skills, such as in preparation for performing a role-play, rather than merely working through worksheets and exercises from the textbook.

Being able to read texts while on the move appeals to boys and girls, although boys are rather more enthusiastic. Consequently, a task such as 'moving around the classroom, matching up town and road signs on the walls with English signs on a list' is much more motivating than simply matching them up on a printed sheet. A task such as this also lends a degree of authenticity to the exercise, although clearly you need to be confident that the class will respond sensibly.

The following strategies and materials allow a degree of interactivity and a multi-skill approach.

Moving and matching

Numbered adverts from newspapers are stuck on cards around the room. These might include an announcement of a birth or engagement, a washing machine for sale, or a lost cat. Pupils must match the numbers with the English translations on a list. Alternatively, pupils match up descriptions of famous people with numbered photos of them stuck on the classroom walls.

Memorizing and adapting text

Having been presented with a short text on the OHP, pupils are challenged to memorize as much of the text as possible within a time limit, say 20 seconds. This can be done with either lists of words, such as menus or shopping lists, or with role-plays such as the one below. This would obviously be presented in the target language:

A: Hello!
B: How are you?
A: I'm fine, thank you. And you?

B: Not bad.
A: Where are you going?
B: I'm going to the cinema.
A: Have fun! Bye!
B: Thanks! Bye!

The teacher then conceals lines, or parts of lines, with strips of paper and reads the text aloud, asking pupils to fill in the gaps chorally. Differentiation is easily achieved: with a lower ability class the teacher conceals only the last word or words of a sentence, or allows pupils to see the first letter of the missing word. With a higher ability class the whole line would be concealed and when the teacher reaches the last line the exercise may be repeated with the text completely concealed and gradually revealed as the pupils guess the lines correctly.

The pupils are then asked to add a number of words to the text in pairs. I selected the words below for one of my Key Stage 4 classes because they were words that the class commonly forgot and that frequently tripped pupils up in the GCSE exam.

really?
perhaps
but
never
wonderful

Each of the words must be used once only, and the pupils can be as creative as they like. When they have completed the writing, pupils read aloud their sketch to the rest of the class. Their classmates are given the task of monitoring that all of the necessary words have been included once only, and the teacher may also ask questions about the context in which they were used. An alternative task involves asking the pupils to add the lines for a third person – a foreign language assistant if the school has one.

Software

Boys are much more motivated to read if the text is accessed via a software package or CD-Rom. Accessing text via an electronic medium makes reading into a more public, rather than private, activity; some research has claimed that insecure boys can react adversely to reading because it necessitates being alienated from their peers. IT makes reading a 'hands-on' activity and offers the additional advantage of satisfying boys' demands for instant feedback. It can also encourage boys to work co-operatively; some of the most successful pairwork that I have seen has involved boys working together at a computer terminal.

The UK market is now awash with innovative software for MFL learning and most textbooks are accompanied by some software. 'Fun with Texts', produced by Camsoft, remains the best-selling MFL software package in the UK. Although it is time-consuming for the teacher to input the text it does allow texts to be used that are directly relevant to the language and topic that pupils are studying. I have also observed boys' classes responding very positively to 'Granville', an old package that is probably lurking at the back of your MFL store cupboard. It allows pupils to explore a virtual French town, selecting activities such as going shopping, eating out or the ever popular visit to the casino.

Selecting appropriate reading materials

The content of readers and textbooks has now begun to accommodate boys' interests much more than in previous years. The Mary Glasgow readers, for example, clearly take boys' interests into account. Unfortunately, the same cannot be said for many GCSE exam papers that still feature fictional texts that are more likely to appeal to girls. It is important that, if possible, you attempt to provide a balance of fictional and factual reading texts to engage both boys and girls and that you try to give pupils a choice if you can. It is also worth buying a copy of one of the *Harry Potter* series in the target language. Extracts from this can be used for all sorts of purposes and pupils are generally very interested in seeing how this enormously popular character is depicted abroad.

Quizzes

When studying the topic of describing where they live pupils are given a multiple-choice quiz to complete about a country or town where the target language is spoken. Here are some examples extracted from a German quiz:

Deutschland Quiz

1. Was sind *Trabbis* und *Wartburgs*? (What are Trabbis and Wartburgs? – old East German cars)
   a) eine schlimme Krankheit
   b) ehemalige ostdeutsche Automarken
   c) wilde Tiere

2. Wo findet man das *Brandenburger Tor*? (Where can you find the Brandenburg Gate?)
   a) unter der Erde
   b) in Berlin
   c) in Prag
   d) in Bonn

3. Was sind die drei Farben der deutschen Fahne? (What are the three colours of the German flag?)
   a) schwarz, rot, blau
   b) schwarz, rot, gelb
   c) schwarz, rot, gold

4. Wer war *Goethe*? (Who was Goethe?)
   a) ein Ministerpräsident
   b) ein Musiker
   c) ein Dichter

5. Was ist die Hauptstadt von Deutschland? (What is the capital of Germany?)
   a) Frankfurt-am-Main
   b) Berlin
   c) München
   d) Bonn

6. Welche dieser Komponisten sind Deutsche? (Which of these composers are German?)
   a) Mozart
   b) Beethoven
   c) Schubert
   d) Holst
   e) Schumann
   f) Mahler
   g) Bach

7. Wo findet das *Oktoberfest* statt? (Where does the Oktoberfest take place?)
   a) Dresden
   b) München
   c) Köln

8. Was ist *Schwarzwälderkirschtorte*? (What is black forest gateau?)
   a) eine Gegend im Schwarzwald
   b) ein leckerer Kuchen
   c) eine Kuh

Pupils complete this, perhaps for homework, using the Internet. A search of this kind helps to train their scanning skills since they will have to search for the key words in texts that contain lots of unknown words. It is worth discussing this strategy with them and making them aware of the fact that they will have to employ a similar strategy in the GCSE Reading Exam. The section 'Training reading skills' presents further ideas on this. The quiz also gives pupils insight into the cultural context of the language that they are studying and, for this reason, is often popular with boys.

When pupils have completed the quiz, and the answers have been given, they are set the task of producing their own quiz about their own home town or country. The completed quizzes are then given to fellow pupils in the class to complete, or to a parallel class.

The questions can also be presented as an exciting 'Who wants to be a millionaire?' quiz, using a Powerpoint presentation. Pupils can then follow this up with their own IT-generated versions and use it to challenge one of their fellow pupils or the teacher.

Language auctions

A language auction can fulfil one of two functions:

1. It can be an entertaining, and constructive, way of highlighting common errors in pupils' work and encouraging them to spot the mistakes themselves. Having marked pupils' written homework the teacher selects a number of sentences from the pupils' work and presents them, numbered 1–10, on an OHT or interactive white-

board. Some of these sentences are perfectly correct while others contain mistakes that a number of the pupils have made. The teacher invites bids in the target language, i.e. 'Who'll give me 2 Euros for sentence number 1?' and the pupils bid for sentences that they think are correct. When the bidding is over the teacher declares whether the sentence was correct or incorrect and either awards the last amount of money bid to the winning pupil, or else deducts it from their 'account'. A pupil accountant can keep a record of the pupils' winnings, or else they can be noted on the board. The class then discuss what was wrong with the incorrect sentence before moving on to the next sentence. This is a motivating way of getting pupils to engage with the work that the teacher has marked and makes summative assessment into a formative assessment opportunity.

2. It can be used to challenge pupils to memorize as many new words as possible. This is a useful extension exercise for quick workers. When pupils have finished noting down new vocabulary they are instructed to remember as many of the words as possible. The teacher then switches off the OHP and instructs pupils to close their books and asks 'Who can give me one word?', 'Who can give me two words?' and so on. The bidding continues until there is only one pupil's hand left in the air (usually a boy's!) when the teacher challenges them to recite those words. The rest of the class are allowed to open their books and monitor the accuracy and number of words given. A prize can be awarded to the pupil who manages to recite the greatest number of words correctly.

Decoding

Boys, in particular, respond very positively to the challenge of unlocking codes. A text in the foreign language is presented with code symbols replacing some of the letters. Pupils must decipher the code and then write out the text correctly. An example is given below:

J'*◆ ✿n ch✳t ☺t ✿n ch◆☺n

Key: all vowels are represented by symbols

a = ✳
u = ✿
e = ☺
i = ◆

They can then create their own encoded texts to present to fellow pupils.

Puzzles and logic problems

Many boys enjoy solving logic problems, so it is worth looking out for puzzle books when you visit a target language country. Older textbooks such as *Le Français d'Aujourd'hui* (Downes, P. and Griffiths, E., (1966) English Universities Press) often contain puzzles which are suitable for higher ability pupils, along with 'Spot the difference' pictures.

A simple reading puzzle can be created by giving pupils a textual description of a room or street. Pupils have to draw the room or street in the empty box above the description, ensuring that all furniture or shops are in the correct places. The text can be made more difficult by including colours, adjectives and comparative forms, e.g. there is a small green rug in the middle of the room; the supermarket is four times bigger than the butcher's shop. Again, pupils can then produce their own written versions to be completed by their peers.

Jokes

Getting pupils to read jokes in the target language can be particularly useful if you are teaching German since it helps to counteract the stereotype that the Germans have no sense of humour! Boys, it seems, also value highly teachers who display a sense of humour. Jokes can be downloaded, being very carefully selective, from a website like *www.306wd.com/deutschjokes/*. They will inevitably elicit comments from the pupils such as 'They're crap!' which is the perfect cue for the teacher to challenge the pupils to produce some funny jokes in the TL. Jokes can also be made into gapped texts, with pupils either having to fill in individual words, or the punch line.

Smudged texts

This is a more entertaining alternative to a gapped text. The teacher presents the class with a text where some of the words or letters are smudged, and so are not legible. The pupils must then reconstruct the original text. An amusing story about how the text came to be smudged makes the task much more appealing. For instance, a text about food is presented with red ketchup blobs on it (red OHT pen or red ink) and the teacher describes how there was an unfortunate spillage at the dinner table the previous evening. A holiday postcard, sent by the teacher to their parents, describes how it was raining every day, and what the teacher was doing on holiday. The rain has, however, smudged some of the text.

'Hands-on' reading tasks

Boys are likely to respond much more positively to reading tasks if they involve some tactile element, i.e. handling materials or moving around. Most worksheet or textbook-based 'matching up' or 'put the sentences in the right order' exercises can easily be adapted so that pupils have to remove the words from an envelope and place them in pairs, or in the correct order, on their desk. 'Miniflashcards', produced by Mary Glasgow are an extremely versatile resource that are intended for use in pairs. They cover a vast range of vocabulary and include suggestions for activities using the cards. 'Putting the sentences/words in the right order' can also be made much more fun if individual pupils are given cards displaying the words and then have to stand in the correct order in front of the rest of the class. The rest of the class decide whether the order is correct.

Matching up exercises can also easily involve moving around the classroom if one part of the pair is stuck on the walls of the classroom so that pupils have to embark on a 'treasure hunt' to find it. This might involve matching pictures of animals with descriptions; pictures of buildings with descriptions of what happens in those buildings. The matching exercise can be made more challenging if the pupils are given an English phrase and have to find both the matching pictures and TL phrase, the pictures and TL phrases have numbers and letters respectively attached to them, and the pupils note these down next to the English phrase, e.g. tourist information office: A 3.

Training reading skills

In interviews boys generally explained their dislike of reading by referring to their non-comprehension of unfamiliar words:

Y9: ... the books don't know what level you're at, and there are words I've never seen before, and it confuses me.

Y7: I don't really like reading because I don't understand what they're saying. Miss has to tell you.

Pupils' frustration at non-comprehension of words is often due to their lack of knowledge or incentive to access unknown vocabulary in dictionaries or glossaries. In class pupils were rarely observed using dictionaries and boys' lack of a logical, pre-formulated strategy to tackle gapped texts was noticed. It would seem that time spent on encouraging and instructing pupils to access unknown vocabulary in a glossary or dictionary is time well spent, even though dictionaries can no longer be used in the GCSE exam. This is an important part of equipping pupils to become independent learners.

The challenge presented by using a dictionary should not be underestimated; pupils are all too easily confused by the array of symbols that follows each word. The following strategies can be used to train pupils' reading skills:

- Presenting pupils with a list of mistakes that other pupils have made when using a dictionary can be an amusing way of training pupils to use this resource effectively, e.g. the teacher asks the pupils, 'What was this pupil trying to say in their restaurant dialogue?', then shows them the incorrect phrase, 'Un élan au chocolat'. The pupils discover that this is a chocolate moose and then have to find the correct word for 'mousse'.

- Competitions with the dictionary: 'The first person to give me the word for ... /a sentence meaning ...'

- Pupils practise their ability to skim read a test by providing a headline or title for an article or text. Alternatively, they practise their predictive skills by reading a title or headline and guessing the keywords that will appear in the text to which it refers.

- Boys are seemingly more motivated to infer the meaning of unknown words from the context, an important reading skill, if they are working through a software package than if they are working from a textbook. They are more motivated to deduce meaning from the context and graphics because progression through the package is dependent on their understanding of these words.

- Refer pupils to the target language that is displayed on the walls to help pupils decipher the meaning of text. It can also be good practice to have target language phrases displayed on the ceiling to catch those leaning back on their chairs!

Reading aloud

Asking pupils to read aloud to the rest of the class allows the teacher to assess pronunciation. However, it should be used with a degree of caution. It is very difficult to try to make sense of a text if one is being asked to read it to an audience and has had no time to prepare it; not understanding the text will obviously affect intonation. It is unfair to ask a pupil to read aloud a text if they have not had this preparation time. Many pupils can be intimidated by having to read aloud and many boys will attempt to conceal their lack of confidence by being silly.

If the teacher reads the text aloud pupils have the time to grapple with the meaning and are aided by the teacher's intonation. They can also be actively engaged in this activity by the teacher pausing and asking them to provide the next word in the text. Alternatively, the pupils must put up their hands whenever the teacher makes a deliberate mistake. These activities can also be done in pairs.

Presenting the written word for the first time

There has been much debate about when is the right time to introduce the written word for the first time to pupils. Many teachers prefer to expose the pupils initially to the visual only, arguing that premature presentation of the written word will confuse pupils and mar their pronunciation. My experience has suggested that some pupils learn more effectively by seeing the written word at the same time as the visual. Some teachers have acted on the same conviction by presenting flashcards and words simultaneously. There is no conclusive answer, but it is always worth consulting the pupils on their preferred learning style.

Reading for pleasure

A number of readers are now available that appeal more to boys' interests by focusing on topics such as factual issues and sport; these include the series published by Mary Glasgow. It is important to purchase readers with boys' preferences for factual materials in mind so that readers do not focus exclusively on fiction.

Pupils can be asked to produce a simple review of readers using the target language. When pupils finish reading a book they complete a card provided by the teacher on which they note the title and author, grade it out of ten, write an opinion word and write a sentence or two summarizing the book. This can then be stuck in their exercise book and/or filed in the front cover of the book for the interest of future readers.

Comics also seemingly appeal to boys much more than girls and some teachers keep a pile of them in the classroom to be used as an extension activity (or treat) for those who finish early.

5 Writing

The problem with writing

Boys seem to encounter many more problems with writing than girls, and this accounts for the negative attitudes to writing frequently expressed by them. Fifty per cent of boys in a sample of 375 claimed that they did not enjoy writing.

Spelling is often identified as the main problem and boys are sometimes embarrassed by untidy handwriting. Boys also criticize writing as being impractical, a view that is sometimes shared by girls:

> If you go to France you're not going to write everything down, are you? It's not really important, writing.
>
> (Year 9 girl)

Both boys and girls claim to experience difficulty in manipulating language when producing independent written work. This latter problem might partially be explained by pupils' association of writing with copying from the board or a textbook. One Year 8 boy described the problem in the following way:

> I don't like writing 'cos you don't know how to put things together. There's little things like 'is' that we'd say, and you don't know the things like that.

Handwriting and spelling

It is all too easy to base assessment of a written piece of work on its appearance; untidy presentation is often equated with poor content. The majority of teachers would agree that boys' work is generally scruffier than girls' and, if they are honest, that this negatively influences their grading of it. This may sound trite, but it is always worth being aware of the fact that neat presentation and sound content do not always go hand-in-hand.

It is worth ensuring that your assessment criteria do not always include presentation, but focus on content instead. This should force you to overlook poor handwriting, as long as it does not render the text illegible. The assessment criteria should always be made clear to pupils in advance, so that they at least have a chance of tidying up their writing if that is going to be assessed.

Some teachers have found that focusing on foreign handwriting gives the pupils a chance to reflect on their own handwriting. Looking at the traditional French style of writing, for example, and setting the pupils the task of reproducing the text in a French style, can provide a valuable opportunity for pupils to focus on their own writing. It also provides an interesting stimulus for discussion of cultural differences. Given that the GCSE examination comprises a number of hand-written texts, it is extremely important that pupils are aware of these differences and are not intimidated by a 'foreign' style.

Making bridges with English

The National Curriculum Programme of Study for Key Stages 3 and 4 suggests under 'Developing language-learning skills' (3c) that:

> Pupils should be taught to use their knowledge of English or another language when learning the target language.
>
> (DfEE and QCA (1999) p.16)

When this version of the National Curriculum was published, I found this to be a heartening addition. The 'chunk-based' approach to teaching and learning language that is perhaps advocated by the bulk of transactional language in the GCSE exam impedes many pupils' progress. Boys often demonstrate an interest in the structure and logical patterns of language, and this statement endorses indulging these interests.

A languages adviser based in the North of England once related a story to me that demonstrates well how pupils' search for patterns in a foreign language can be impeded by learning chunks of language. He was observing a French lesson in which the class were practising how to say whether they had any brothers or sisters. After some whole-class spoken practice the class was divided into pairs to continue. The adviser approached two boys and asked them which word in the question they were asking, 'As-tu des frères ou des soeurs?', meant 'brothers'. The two put their heads together and, counting on their fingers, worked out that the word for brothers in the equivalent English question, 'Have you got any brothers or sisters?' was the fifth word. They therefore reasoned that the fifth word in the French question, 'ou' had to be the word for 'brothers'.

This account indicates the need to allow pupils to analyse the chunks of language that we teach them. We need to break these chunks down into their constituent lexical parts so that pupils are able to translate and use individual words. This might allow pupils to learn the 'little things like "is" ', referred to in the Year 8 boy's words earlier, and use them competently in their independent written work.

IT

Letter writing, a staple ingredient of the GCSE writing paper, seems to appeal much more to girls than to boys. Boys are not as motivated by the prospect of a tangible outcome of their writing, in the form of a return letter, as one might expect. Girls are much keener: in response to a questionnaire, 43 per cent of Year 8 girls claimed they would 'enjoy a lot' writing a letter which their teacher was going to send to France, Germany or Spain compared with only 23 per cent of the boys. Girls are seemingly much more likely to write letters to friends and penfriends in their free time, so for many boys writing a letter in a foreign language may be a first-time experience.

What makes a difference to the intrinsic interest of writing a letter is if it is word-processed. Even a relatively mundane task such as 'writing a postcard' takes on fresh appeal if pupils are allowed to complete it electronically. This task, 'writing a postcard using a computer', appeared on the same questionnaire and received a much more positive response from the boys.

IT offers numerous advantages where writing is concerned. It removes the embarrassment of poor handwriting and spelling and makes writing less private. It makes the prospect of editing and re-drafting less of an anathema to boys, and, as previously stated in Chapter 4, boys are more responsive to instantaneous correction by a computer.

Research conducted by Ofsted has found that computers are underused by MFL teachers and that where they are used appropriately they can have a significant effect on pupils' motivation, particularly boys'. I suspect that one of the reasons for this underuse is that MFL teachers quite simply find it difficult to book a computer suite when they are in competition with their colleagues from other subjects. There may, however, be another reason that is linked to anxiety generated by the expectation that using ICT to teach MFL has to involve using complex software. This is clearly not the case. Simple word processing offers a myriad of motivating opportunities for writing exercises, not least to create writing frameworks. These are now commonly used in the Literacy Strategy in primary schools and offer boys the structure that is so often lacking in their written work. Some applications of word-processed texts are listed below:

- The teacher saves electronically a number of target language questions relating to holidays, e.g. Where did you go on holiday last year? Who did you go with? What was the weather like? What was the food like? The pupils set about word-processing their answers to these questions. When they have answered each question they can delete it. This is likely to encourage boys to produce a much more extended piece of written work than they would have done without the framework. It also gives pupils a sense of satisfaction and progress when they can delete the questions that they have answered.

- The pupils are instructed to underline all the verbs in a text that the teacher has previously saved. Alternatively, they could change the verbs into another tense, for instance from perfect to future tense.

- The pupils have to change a text from the first person into the third person. This could be placed in a fictitious, 'authentic' context such as placing the pupils in the role of a police officer who has to write up a witness statement of a car accident from the original statement given by an onlooker. Pupils would have to change the verb forms in sentences like 'I was walking down the street at 2 o'clock' into '(S)he was walking down the street at 2 o'clock.'

- Pupils first have to highlight in bold, then change all of the adjectives in a text. They could either choose the adjectives themselves or be instructed to replace them with the opposites. A list of such opposites is given below. This can be a particularly useful, and fun, exercise with Key Stage 4 groups who often forget the all-important 'little words'.

Gegenteile (Opposites)
   schwarz (black) –
   nein (no) –
   hell (bright/light) –
   intelligent –
   reich (rich) –
   groß (big/tall) –
   schlank (thin) –
   teuer (expensive) –
   schön (beautiful) –
   kalt (cold) –
   gut (good) –
   laut (loud) –
   schwer (difficult/heavy) –
   lang (long) –
   interessant (interesting) –
   schnell (quick) –
   immer (always) –

- Pupils are given the first half of a story or dialogue and have to write the ending. The alternative endings, after being marked by the teacher, are circulated among the whole class who vote for the best one.

- More able pupils write headlines or titles for pictures that the teacher has downloaded from the Internet and saved electronically.

- Gap-filling exercises become much more engaging on a computer screen, particularly if pupils are instructed how to use an online dictionary.

- Putting the lines of a dialogue or story in the correct order. Virtual cutting and pasting is much more engaging for pupils then simply writing them out, and much less time-consuming for the teacher than cutting up strips of paper with the phrases on them for the pupils to re-arrange on their desks.

- Pupils produce a Powerpoint presentation on a topic such as 'My home town'. These could be emailed to the teacher for marking. The best presentations are selected by the teacher and presented by the pupils to the rest of the class. This activity could be linked with the first activity in this list, with the pupils' answers to each question forming the basis of one slide.

Visuals and drama

Many boys view writing as a passive, impractical activity, so tasks like 'writing a description of yourself' generally appeal much more to girls. Activities involving visuals or drama, such as designing cartoons or posters, or writing role-plays to be performed, are perceived as highly motivating: 65 per cent of the boys in single-sex groups claimed to enjoy 'designing your own cartoon in French', compared with 47 per cent of the girls. Many boys enjoy writing role-plays because they can be creative and because the writing has a purpose; they will perform it.

> I enjoy it when we do practical stuff like plays and someone has to read out their things and that. I don't like it when we're just, like, writing things out.
>
> (Year 10 boy)

I have seen some excellent examples of written work on posters; this format, it seems, is of particular appeal to boys. It is important, however, that a minimum number of words is stipulated to avoid the poster being dominated by pictures. This applies equally to posters that are created using ICT. Very often electronically generated posters are created through ICT for aesthetic purposes only – to create wonderfully illustrated work. While this may enhance pupils' ability to use a computer, it adds little to their achievement in MFL.

It is always worth collecting pictures, and series of pictures – humorous, shocking or thought-provoking – to use as a stimulus for writing. The following activities could be used with a series of pictures:

- Pupils are shown the first picture and predict what will happen in the second, and so on.

- Pupils add a title and/or speech bubbles.

- Memory game: pupils are shown the pictures briefly and then write an account of what happened in the story, including as much detail as possible.

- Pupils invent an alternative ending.

Finding an audience

Having an audience, or recipient, for pupils' written work is probably the best way of increasing motivation, especially where boys are concerned. An email partner in the form of an exchange school in a target language country presents all sorts of opportunities, not least the opportunity for pupils to 'use the target language for real purposes' (National Curriculum Programme of Study, 5h). Instrumentally motivated boys are much more likely to want to learn how to ask what someone does in their free time in a foreign language if they know that they will need the question to gain this information from an email partner. Email has a distinct advantage over snail mail in terms of speed, although email exchanges are equally dependent on the writers' diligence. At their best, email exchanges can provide a real forum in which to apply new language, although synchronizing curriculum content with the content of emails can be difficult if pupils' partners are tardy respondents. The CILT book, *E-mail: Using electronic communications in foreign language teaching* (1997) by Kate Townshend, provides some excellent ideas for making the most of email exchanges. Email partner schools can be found via contact with the local council, who may have an exchange with another town or city, via ALL who sometimes advertise schools abroad seeking UK partners in their newsletter, or via the website, *www.epals.com*.

In the absence of a partner abroad, a neighbouring school, or a parallel class within the same school, can be an equally worthy audience. One of the teachers in a case-study school had her Year 10 boys' class completing dating agency forms in French on St Valentine's day. These were then exchanged with the parallel girls' group and the pupils selected their ideal partners. This led on to pupils writing letters of introduction to each other, embellishing their descriptions as they liked. This proved a highly effective way of getting pupils to write letters for a real, and entertaining, purpose. It can also be sustained, in the same way as an email exchange, with pupils applying the new language, as they acquire it, in a letter. This renders much easier the onerous task faced by the teacher of having to justify to the pupils why the language is relevant to them. The pupils' interest can be further fuelled if they keep their identities secret and take on a fictitious persona. Boys, in particular, are much more likely to write more if they are not writing about themselves, but their hero. The correspondence could also incorporate quizzes, puzzles and surveys created by the pupils.

Correspondence such as this can also involve preparing video recordings; classes are always keen on seeing other pupils perform. Simply informing pupils that the restaurant role-plays they write will be videoed to be shown to an audience creates a purpose. Alternatively, classes could write playscripts for each other and then view their play being performed on video tape by the actors.

As a follow-on activity each pupil, or pair of pupils, could be asked to produce a written review of one of the role-plays which is then sent back to the pupil who produced it. The teacher would need to define the assessment criteria, which could look something like the following:

Film review – Im Café

Folgendes hat mir gefallen: (I liked the following)

. . . .
. . . .
. . . .

Wortschatz (Vocabulary):

Aussprache (Pronunciation):

This type of activity is in line with the Key Stage 3 Strategy's 'peer assessment' which it sets out to promote. The pupils would need the teacher's input in order to complete the review form but differentiation is easily accommodated. Less able, and younger, pupils could select their verdicts from a range of judgements provided by the teacher on the form and add their own simple opinion words, while Key Stage 4 pupils could be exposed to the GCSE criteria used to mark the presentation part of the speaking test.

Younger or older classes within your school can also provide a readership for short books or comic strips that pupils produce as a writing exercise. Small books are still very much in vogue in bookshops at the moment, and the teacher could validate the exercise by bringing in some examples, preferably in the TL. Children's books in the TL present an excellent model for sixth-form or higher ability classes at Key Stage 4. Students in these classes could be tasked with writing a book for younger pupils along the lines of the *Mr Men* series, having read a few of the *Mr Men* books in the TL. Younger classes could easily produce a simple book that is tied together with ribbon. Such books could describe the daily routine of a famous person, perhaps someone who speaks the TL. The name of the person could be withheld until the last page, leaving the reader to guess their identity.

Creative writing

Boys claim to enjoy writing creatively about their interests much more than completing formal writing tasks such as reading comprehensions. Below are a number of ideas for getting pupils to write creatively:

- Poetry. The complexity of the language in a poem can vary enormously to suit the pupils' level. Emblem poems are a good way of motivating younger children and can be an excellent way of facilitating memorization. A simple example of a poem representing a mountain is given here:

RBERG
EBERGBERG
GBERGBERGBERG
IBERGBERGBERGBERG
EBERGBERGBERGBERGBERG
TBERGBERGBERGBERGBERGBERG
SBERGBERGBERGBERGBERGBERGBERG

They can also incorporate hidden words to make them more engaging. The more observant reader will have noticed the mountain climber (Steiger) ascending the left-hand slope!

Acrostic poems can contribute to pupils' knowledge of adjectives and can consolidate instruction on how to use a dictionary. The name 'Louise', for instance, could be made into an acrostic poem in the following way:

Liebevoll (loving)
Original
Und (and)
Intelligent
Super
Elegant

Poems can also be a good way of practising different tense forms. Pupils can be asked to reflect on their lives as children, and compare this with their current situation, in order to complete a poem along the following lines:

Quand j'avais quatre ans j'étais joyeuse
Quand j'avais six ans j'étais malheureuse
Quand j'avais dix ans j'étais petite
Maintenant je suis grande.

An added incentive to write poetry can be provided by submitting pupils' entries to a poetry competition. This could either be run in school or else it is worth contacting ALL to establish whether your regional branch is organizing a competition. Details of one poetry and song competition can be found at *www.cilt.org.uk/comenius/briscom.htm#free/*

- Challenge pupils to write as long a sentence as possible by taking it in turns to add one word, or phrase, at a time to a short core sentence. This is particularly useful for practising separable verbs in German, where the prefix ends up at the end of the sentence. The teacher would write on the board, for example:

- Ich sehe fern. (I watch TV)

Pupils could make this longer in the following way:

- Ich sehe gern fern. (I like watching TV).
- Ich sehe gern um sechs Uhr fern. (I like watching TV at six o'clock).
- Ich sehe gern um sechs Uhr im Wohnzimmer fern. (I like watching TV at six o'clock in the lounge).

An example in French could be:

- Je sors.
- Je sors maintenant.
- Je sors maintenant parce que
- Je sors maintentat parce qu'il y a . . .

This exercise is useful as it stimulates boys to extend their sentences, rather than producing the minimum that many boys produce. It can either be undertaken as a whole-class exercise, with groups competing against each other to extend the sentence written on the board or OHP, or else pupils could tackle it individually, demonstrating each stage of the sentence-writing.

- Soap operas. A number of the current BBC language programmes, such as 'Deutsch Plus' are based on the soap opera format and in my experience this proves very popular with students. 'L'Immeuble' or 'Der Wohnblock', published by Mary Glasgow, gets pupils to create their own soap opera characters, writing love letters to each other, problem letters and postcards from their holiday. This is another good way of getting round the apparent male aversion to letter writing. You might decide to make the whole language-learning experience into a soap opera, with the class being given new identities as characters in the soap and writing wholly from the perspective of their character. As stated in Chapter 2, boys are much more likely to produce more TL in the guise of someone else than as themselves.

- 'Through the Keyhole'. While girls may be happier to discuss the contents of their bedrooms with each other in their first language, this is a topic that rarely features in boys' conversations. Boys are unlikely to be motivated to write a description of their room in the target language. Present the pupils with a model description of the room of a famous person and ask them to guess whose room this is. If you are feeling brave you could even attempt to read it out in the TL with a Loyd Grossman accent! In a text I gave to my students a few years ago the room had a stained dress hanging up and a copy of a book. They guessed quite easily that the room belonged to Monica Lewinsky, who was in the news at the time. Having completed this information-gap exercise, and with their model text in hand, pupils then write their own description of a room and bring it back to class for the others to guess whose room this is.

- At the end of the lesson pupils are set a quick challenge that enables them to review what has been learned. They are asked to write down their own first name, or that of a favourite film or pop star, vertically, as in an acrostic poem. They must then set about making each letter of the name into a word relating to what they have learned in the lesson.

- Graffiti wall. Part of a noticeboard or wallspace is designated a 'Graffiti wall'. Each week pupils are invited to write on the wall, as creatively as they like, the class's favourite word or phrase – the 'word of the week' that has been learned that week.

- 'Consequences' game. This is based on the party game and can be used to practise verbs in the past tense, dates and times. Pupils are each given a blank sheet of A4 paper. At the top of the paper they secretly write a date and/or time, such as 'On the 30th April 2002 at five past five'. They then fold the paper over so that it conceals the date they have written and pass their paper onto their neighbour. On their new sheet of paper they write the name of a famous man. It is important that they do not unfold the paper so that the date remains secret. Again, they fold the paper over and pass it on their neighbour. The game continues in this way with the pupils adding the following details in this order: the name of a famous woman; an activity in the past, such as 'went swimming', 'went to a restaurant', 'went water skiing', and finally a place, such as 'New York' or 'in the pub'. Having passed their papers on for a final time, they are invited to unfold the paper and read out their text. The resultant texts are usually a great source of hilarity, particularly if you are nominated as the famous man or woman. Pupils can then be invited to write up an accurate version of this text, or to amend it to make it more amusing.

- Diaries. To consolidate work on the past tense, and everyday routines, pupils write a diary for one week. This is first written in draft form so that the teacher can draw pupils' attention to errors. An accurate second draft can then be produced, complete with illustrations and realia such as cinema tickets, and bound together with ribbon. The diaries can then be circulated to the class who guess who has written the diary they are reading. Pupils could also be asked to write up, or read out, the diary in the third person, e.g. 'Il est allé ...'

- Problem-page letters. More able pupils or students in the sixth-form could be asked to write, and respond to, problem-page letters. Problem letters also provide stimulating reading comprehension or gap-filling materials for less able or younger pupils.

- Writing a story from a list of words. This is a group activity. Each group is given an envelope with a number of words or phrases on cards inside it. Each individual takes it in turn to remove a card and has to say a sentence that contains the word or phrase. The sentences must link together to create a story. When each card has been used the group sets about writing up their story which can then be read to the rest of the class and the best story selected. Alternatively, when the stories have been corrected, the group sets about creating a reading comprehension which they set as a challenge to a neighbouring group. This is a good exercise for more able pupils to practise question forms.

Writing independently or avoiding 'Copiez les mots'

The National Curriculum level descriptions indicate that, ultimately, what we should be aiming to develop in our pupils is an ability to write independently. This progression is summarized with reference to the National Curriculum levels below:

Level 1 – copy and label
Level 2 – copy phrases
Level 3 – write short phrases from memory
Level 4 – write paragraphs with appropriate use of dictionaries and glossaries
Level 5 – beginning to apply basic elements of grammar
Level 6 – use both informal and formal styles of writing
Level 7 – edit and redraft
Level 8 – express and justify ideas ... spelling and grammar are generally accurate
Exceptional Performance – a wide range of factual and imaginative topics ... vary the style and scope of their writing.

While we cannot expect all of our pupils to attain the lofty heights of exceptional performance, it is important to note that even at Level 3 pupils are expected to begin manipulating language independently. It is all too easy to fall into the 'Copiez les mots' trap; whenever pupils are introduced to new vocabulary instinct tells you that their next task should be to copy them out.

When time is short, and your workload excessive, this practice may be inevitable. However, it is always worth considering how a copying task could be made a little more challenging, involving the pupils in true writing rather than simply copying. You should also think about why you are asking pupils to copy these phrases. It might be because you believe that the process of writing down the words progresses pupils' learning; it helps pupils to familiarize themselves with the written form of the words they have just heard and spoken. If this is the case, then remember that copying actually involves very little intellectual exercise. Rather, it is more a case of pupils being able to demonstrate their co-ordination skills, in moving their eyes to and from the board, or the textbook, and back to their book. The National Curriculum levels indicate the lack of intellectual stimulus this offers: this is a Level 2 task.

Most likely, your reason for asking the pupils to copy vocabulary is that they need to have an accurate written record of these new words. Ideally, writing should both provide pupils with this record and challenge them cognitively. A simple modification to the original 'Copiez les mots' task can achieve this.

Imagine that you are introducing your class to weather phrases. You use flashcards to practise these, and a range of flashcard exercises such as those described in Chapter 2. Now you want the pupils to write up these phrases. Setting one of the following simple tasks would ensure that the writing stage does not merely involve copying:

- pupils match up flashcard pictures (stuck on the board) with phrases displayed on the OHP or on a worksheet

- pupils match up the new TL phrases and English phrases, either on a worksheet, or displayed on the OHP or whiteboard

- pupils reconstruct the words from simple anagrams

- pupils are given incomplete phrases, either on a worksheet or displayed to the whole class, and have to fill in the gaps. The missing letters or words should be words which they have come across before, or which you anticipate that they will find unproblematic. In French, for instance, gaps could be as follows:

  - _ _ neige.
  - Il _ _ _ _ du brouillard.
  - Il _ leut.

Examples in German could be:

- _ _ _ Sonne scheint.
- Es _ _ _ kalt.
- Es ist _ olkig.

The other advantage of this approach is that it focuses pupils' attention on the interrelationship of sounds and writing in the target language (Programme of Study 1a). Their ability to use the language independently will progress slowly if they are not given opportunities to do this.

This is perhaps why *dictation* has returned to many MFL classrooms, having been resurrected from 'O' level pedagogy. Many teachers now recognize it as a potentially valuable exercise that allows pupils to make connections between sounds and writing. It can also give the teacher access to common errors and misunderstandings. Dictation should not just be seen as a means of summative assessment, as perhaps it was in 'O' level days. It can be used in formative assessment as well, to further pupils' learning. If used to this end, it is important that you offer the pupils an accurate written model so that they can mark their own, or each other's work, and learn from their mistakes. Collecting in pupils' written dictations to mark would deprive them of this learning opportunity and provide you with summative performance data only.

An increasing number of MFL departments are discovering the delights of an even more historic resource: the slate. The contemporary version of the slate is known as a *'show-me' board*. They are exercise book-size whiteboards on which the pupils write with erasable ink pens. These are excellent for promoting pupils' basic writing skills in an enjoyable way and can be used for a multitude of functions. When the teacher asks a question, the pupils write their answers on their boards and then display them to the teacher. This gives the teacher instant access to all pupils' responses, enabling them to pick out common mistakes. It also means that writing becomes less of a private activity which, as mentioned before, is likely to make it more popular with boys.

'Show-me boards' can help to adjust the balance of a lesson that is heavily speaking-oriented and can encourage pupils to experiment with their writing. They can be used in the early stages of introducing new vocabulary to challenge the pupils to anticipate what the written form might look like, rather than deferring pupils' exposure to the written word until later. It is a good idea to keep the boards in plastic seal-tight transparent bags together with two coloured pens and a cloth. The boards can be obtained from the following company: Compass, Waveney Drive, Lowestoft NR33 0YX. Telephone: 01502 500444.

Coursework

Many schools now choose to enter their pupils for written coursework at GCSE level instead of for the terminal written examination. Some of the teachers in my study reported that boys were much more motivated by coursework as it gave them a chance to write about a topic of interest to them. The Year 10 boys' teacher found that his class of boys were particularly motivated by a description of a football match. This was produced around the time of the World Cup, and the teacher was especially pleased with the length of the work which, in many cases, exceeded the word limit stipulated by the exam board. Other teachers experienced quite the opposite, finding, as is so often the case, that boys' coursework was excessively brief and careless. If pupils are to produce successful coursework, they clearly need careful preparation and a structure on which to base their work.

Below are some tips that you might like to bear in mind about coursework. They are derived from Julie Adams's Pathfinder, *On Course for GCSE Coursework*, published by CILT. It contains lots of useful advice.

Tips for successful coursework

- Prepare pupils for coursework by giving them practice tasks beforehand.

- Give constructive feedback on these practice pieces.

- Pupils must be competent dictionary users.

- Pupils may be encouraged to make use of work already carried out in other subjects.

- Give pupils a 'coursework planner'.

- Pupils need to know how coursework will be marked.

- Encourage pupils at Key Stage 3 to create a portfolio of written work.

6 Teaching and learning styles

Tuning into pupils' interests and learning styles

When interviewed, pupils make it clear that what makes the most difference to whether or not they enjoy and do well in languages is not the sex of the teacher, or whether they are in a single-sex class, but how their teacher teaches them. Teachers who make conscious efforts to tune into pupils' interests and learning styles, and make this clear to the class in their planning, enjoy greater success.

Using the following questionnaire as a precursor to group discussion will give you a broad insight into how your pupils learn. Completing it yourself is also useful as it should help you to reflect on how your own preferred learning style informs your teaching style. In order to accommodate all pupils' learning styles it is clearly important that we try to ensure that our teaching is not wholly driven by our own preferences.

Myself as a learner

1. I learn quickly when . . . .
   . . . .
2. I learn slowly when. . . . .
   . . . .
3. I learn easily when . . . .
   . . . .
4. Learning in groups. . . . .
   . . . .
5. I learn well from someone who . . . .
   . . . .
6. I enjoy learning when. . . . .
   . . . .
7. Learning from books. . . . .
   . . . .

Where boys are concerned, sport often features highly in their interests. One teacher I worked with made the Tour de France a central feature of her lessons in July. The route of the Tour was mapped out on one wall of her classroom and at the beginning of each lesson the class would discuss who had won the yellow jersey during the previous stage. Profiles of the cyclists were written, and the towns that the cyclists were passing through were studied; this provides much more interesting cultural subject matter than studying one's own town.

Another teacher put aside a few minutes at the beginning of each lesson to discuss in French recent football matches, sponsorship and individual players. Numbers can be presented, and practised, in relation to football or basketball scores.

Below is a learning styles questionnaire which can be used to audit pupils' learning preferences in MFL. This can usefully be handed to pupils at the start of a term or year with an explanation that the results will be used to inform the teacher's planning. The teacher then analyses the responses and uses the questionnaire to justify their inclusion of certain activities in lessons, for instance, 'In the questionnaire you told me that you found listening very difficult. So, today, we're going to have a go at a listening exercise and we're going to break it down into stages so that we can think about how listening can be made easier.' Pupils generally respond very positively to teachers personalizing the lesson in this way and appreciate the effort that teachers make when they gear the lesson content to take pupils' views into account.

Analysis of the questionnaire does not require a high level of competence in statistical analysis; percentages are all that are needed to give the teacher a general picture. The most important thing is that pupils see that the teacher is prioritizing their interests.

Learning styles and interests
Which of the following activities do you enjoy or do you think you would enjoy in French lessons?

Tick the box that best describes your feelings about each. Unless you are told otherwise all of the activities are carried out in French.

	enjoy	don't mind	dislike
• speaking	☐	☐	☐
• listening	☐	☐	☐
• reading	☐	☐	☐
• writing	☐	☐	☐
• acting out a role-play	☐	☐	☐
• moving around the class, interviewing others	☐	☐	☐
• answering the teacher's questions	☐	☐	☐
• playing games with flashcards	☐	☐	☐
• following directions from a tape to find a building on a map	☐	☐	☐
• listening to a tape and filling in a grid	☐	☐	☐
• games, e.g. hangman, bingo	☐	☐	☐
• watching videos	☐	☐	☐
• listening to a description of someone wanted by the police and drawing that person	☐	☐	☐
• reading cartoons/comics	☐	☐	☐
• moving around the classroom, matching up signs on the walls with English signs on a list	☐	☐	☐
• using the computer to play games	☐	☐	☐
• reading about the different way of life in France	☐	☐	☐
• putting the lines of a conversation into the right order	☐	☐	☐
• writing a letter to a hotel in France	☐	☐	☐
• designing your own cartoon in French	☐	☐	☐
• using the computer to write a letter	☐	☐	☐
• writing a description of yourself	☐	☐	☐

- writing answers to questions
  about a letter   ☐ ☐ ☐
- writing a role-play with a partner   ☐ ☐ ☐
- writing a letter which your teacher
  is going to send to France   ☐ ☐ ☐
- learning about French grammar   ☐ ☐ ☐
- working on my own   ☐ ☐ ☐
- working with a partner   ☐ ☐ ☐
- working in a group   ☐ ☐ ☐
- using worksheets
- working from a textbook   ☐ ☐ ☐
- lessons in which the teacher
  speaks mainly French   ☐ ☐ ☐

If you had some say in how French was taught, what would you do more often?

. . . .
. . . .
. . . .
. . . .

In your opinion, which of the following things are important for a pupil who wants to do well in French?

	important	not sure	not important
being in all-boys'/-girls' group	☐	☐	☐
being in a group where everyone is of the same ability	☐	☐	☐
being in quite a small class	☐	☐	☐
having a teacher with a good sense of humour	☐	☐	☐
being in a group with your friends	☐	☐	☐
having regular tests	☐	☐	☐
looking good in front of the rest of the class	☐	☐	☐
having a good relationship with the teacher	☐	☐	☐
getting homework regularly	☐	☐	☐

- doing homework on time   ☐   ☐   ☐
- the time of the lesson
  (i.e. morning or afternoon)   ☐   ☐   ☐
- knowing that you'll use your
  French in the future   ☐   ☐   ☐
- competing with other pupils   ☐   ☐   ☐
- the teacher explaining the aims
  of the lesson at the start   ☐   ☐   ☐

Independent learning

In my study, both boys and girls seemed to favour working in pairs or groups rather than on their own. In interviews girls appeared more confident that they were able to work effectively in groups, pointing out that they preferred to be quietly corrected by a partner than by the teacher in front of the class. In contrast, boys sometimes demonstrated an awareness of not working well in groups, as a group of Year 8 boys admitted.

AB: Do you prefer speaking to the teacher or speaking in pairs or groups?

M: Speaking to the teacher.

S: Yeh, 'cos if we're in groups everyone tends to just cheat and. . .

[*Some laughter, general agreement*]

D: The teacher knows what you're saying and people in your class only know as much French as you do, so they just. . .

S: They can't really correct you.

Research on interactional styles has shown that boys are generally not good turn-takers, that they interrupt and dominate group discussions more readily than girls. It is therefore worth thinking about how boys can be trained to contribute considerately to group discussions. One idea, mentioned in Chapter 3, is to give each group an object, such as a ball or a wooden spoon, which must be held by the person who is speaking. A pupil is not allowed to contribute if they are not holding the object.

While boys often seem to be heavily dependent on the teacher they also value being allowed to work independently. It is interesting that boys in interviews frequently chose as their favourites those school subjects which are less tightly structured by the teacher and may allow pupils to work at their own pace and enjoy some freedom of movement, such as art, technology, music, drama and PE. The higher-ability Year 9 boys I observed worked most conscientiously and sensibly on tasks which were not strictly teacher-directed, such as writing and producing display work. One Year 7 boy qualified his claim to have enjoyed working in the computer room by adding:

> But it would help if she didn't walk around saying 'You've done that wrong!' It'd be better if she'd just sit down and let us get on with it.

It is important that we provide pupils with opportunities to learn independently. This is necessary both to boost motivation and to give them a chance of achieving a higher grade. Spoon-feeding is perhaps more of a temptation for MFL teachers than for other teachers, since in a classroom situation the teacher cannot avoid playing a central role at the beginning of the language learning process. In other subjects – history, business studies, mathematics – pupils can be referred to other resources to direct their learning. In MFL the teacher is initially the pupils' principal resource because other resources are not easily accessible. We should be wary of the limitations of spoon-feeding, however, as a well-known author pointed out:

> 'Spoon feeding in the long run teaches us nothing but the shape of the spoon'
>
> E.M. Forster, 1951

Below are some strategies and resources which might help you to incorporate more independent learning opportunities in your lessons:

Examples of activities promoting independent learning

- Pupils take on the role of the teacher, in pairs, groups or with the whole class.

- Project work, for instance preparing a display about a town or city in a target-language country.

- Pupils are given a choice of exercises, or decide on the order in which they will tackle them.

- Listening/reading for pleasure.

- Pupils evaluate each others' work.

- Carousels, i.e. pupils move in groups from one activity to another during the lesson. Ten minutes might be spent on a listening task, ten minutes on a reading task and so on.

- Poster work.

- Recording themselves on audio tape.

- Predicting the theme of the lesson/reading text.

Useful resources for independent learning

- Dictionaries and reference materials which pupils know how to use.

- TL instructions and phrases displayed around the room. It is important that the teacher makes active use of these, referring the pupils to them when their questions can be answered by reading these posters. In this way pupils are encouraged to find the answers themselves rather than instinctively resorting to the teacher.

- Helpsheets giving advice/examples on common areas of difficulty.

- An 'advice desk' – perhaps manned by a pupil or the FLA?

- A colour-coded index (stuck in the front of pupils' exercise books?) indicating the content of their exercise book, and where information can be found in the textbook.

- A flexible classroom layout.

Textbooks

Boys, in particular, often respond negatively to using textbooks excessively. When boys were observed using textbooks in class they generally worked well when the exercise was only one of a series of activities in that lesson, and had to be completed to a deadline, and considerably less well when the exercise lasted all lesson. It is also worth considering consulting the pupils when you are selecting a new textbook to purchase.

'Learn these 10 words for a test': revision

It seems that boys do often respond well to having the discipline of a test imposed on them; 55 per cent of the boys in the three single-sex groups agreed that 'having regular tests' was important. This point was often borne out in interviews with boys' reluctant admission of their necessity:

> *(Year 8)*: I don't like them but they make you remember.
> *(Year 9)*: Having regular tests [is important]. I don't like them but it would make you learn better.

How the test is presented by the teacher is important, however. Where I saw tests being used successfully, the teachers placed great emphasis on pupils' performance in these tests, and the accuracy with which words were written. The tests developed into lively competitions between the boys, with merits being awarded for the best marks. Some class time was also given over to discussing boys' performance in these tests and guidance given on how to prepare for them.

This latter point is of particular importance for boys who, unlike girls, very often have little idea of how to go about revising for a test. Given the frequency with which MFL teachers task pupils with revising new vocabulary for homework, it is worth setting aside some time to discuss possible revision strategies with pupils.

Ernesto Macaro's book *Learning Strategies in foreign and second language classrooms* (Continuum, 2001) offers much useful advice for getting pupils to explore and experiment with the range of learning strategies available to them. One approach to try out is to ask pupils during the lesson after they have been set a test how they went about revising. You can list the strategies they employed and brainstorm some others, perhaps including:

- mnemonics. A mnemonic for remembering German conjunctions that do not send the verb to the end, for instance, could be:
  A (aber)
  U (und)
  S (sondern)
  O (oder)
  D (denn)

- mind-mapping/spider diagrams in which the central word is placed in the centre of the page and related words branch off around this word. This is useful for those pupils who remember words by memorizing their location on a page

- rhyming

- visual connections – words are connected with pictures

- chanting

- saving words electronically

- the 'traditional' way of revising: draw a line down the centre of the page and write English words on one side and TL words on the other. Are pupils aware that it is easier to cover up the TL words first, and see if they can remember the translation from the English, rather than the other way round?

- someone else, such as a parent or sibling, tests the pupil

- making use of cognates

- colour-coding to indicate gender

- recording onto a tape and listening to it before going to sleep

This sort of exercise helps pupils to learn how to learn MFL, an area which we perhaps currently neglect. Following the discussion, you could encourage pupils to try out a different strategy when preparing for the next test, and ensure that the discussion of revision skills is ongoing.

Competing

Boys' competitiveness is frequently cited as an important characteristic which can be exploited in teaching. A considerable number of the teachers of all-boys' groups described capitalizing on the boys' interest in the progress of the parallel all-girls' groups; competitions in singing and grammar and vocabulary knowledge were organized and perceived by teachers to be highly motivating, particularly for the boys. Boys in interviews often mentioned their interest in knowing how the girls were progressing and were keen not to fall behind.

However, observation suggested that the older the boys the less keen they were to compete with each other. And, clearly, if these competitive tendencies are not strictly managed and not counter-balanced by the teacher, rewarding pupils for skills often associated with females, such as lending equipment to each other, not laughing at each other's errors, and offering mutual support, then the competitiveness can become aggressiveness.

The sex of the teacher

Teachers are often keen to know whether their own gender affects their pupils' attitudes to learning MFL. This is clearly a question that cannot be ignored given the preponderance of female MFL staff. 52 per cent of the 799 pupils who responded to one questionnaire had no experience of being taught by a male teacher. Conversely, only 4 per cent had only ever been taught by males.

Most pupils are, it seems, not convinced of the benefits of being taught by a teacher of the same sex as themselves. 47 per cent of pupils who responded to this questionnaire disagreed with the statement 'It's better to be taught by a teacher of the same sex as yourself' and 36 per cent were unsure. In interviews a considerable number claimed to perceive no difference between being taught by male and female teachers, some insisting that there were greater differences between individual teachers regardless of their sex, and that it was the quality of their teaching that mattered:

> Boy (Year 9): It's different teachers, not just different sex teachers, it's just different teachers really.

Boy (Year 9): I've been taught by two women in French and I would just accept a man to teach us. I'm not bothered. I don't think there'd be any change. It's if you're being teached [*sic*] good. . . . Not just like make everyone sit and give you a big lecture. They actually teach, they do games and all that . . .

We should bear in mind, however, that pupils' initial answers may be determined by their reluctance to be seen as sexist. Some pupils in interviews who initially denied any differences in the teaching approaches of males and females subsequently went on to describe some.

The question is obviously a complex and sensitive one. In my experience schools have appointed candidates on the basis of their gender alone, a practice which cannot be condoned but understood if the school has a deficit of male role models. Personally I would argue that one's personality is inextricably linked with gender, and that the teacher's gender invariably influences the way in which they teach. It is only one of many variables that shapes their teaching style. It would also be naive to assume that pupils behave in exactly the same way towards male and female adults; research has demonstrated that infants differentiate between the sexes from a very early age. The following chapter looks further at how the sex of the teacher may play a much more important role in a single-sex class, where pupils' awareness of the teacher's gender is heightened.

7 The teaching and learning environment

This chapter begins by evaluating the effectiveness of teaching foreign languages in single-sex classes. Single-sex grouping has grown in popularity over the last few years, with a significant number of schools setting up single-sex groups in an attempt to raise boys' achievement in English and MFL. This evaluation is based on data I collected from five schools around the country who were piloting such initiatives. This part of the chapter seeks to answer the questions that many MFL teachers have concerning the effectiveness of such groupings, and both pupils' and teachers' views are considered. Other factors that affect the learning environment are discussed in later sections.

There is now considerable evidence to suggest that male and female pupils in single-sex schools have a more positive attitude to subjects traditionally favoured by the opposite sex. In contrast, pupils in co-educational schools tend to conform to sex-stereotypical perceptions of subjects and to pupils favouring subjects which reaffirm their perceived sex role. Modern foreign languages has been singled out by researchers as the subject area in which there is a marked difference between the attitudes and performance of boys in single-sex schools and those in co-educational schools. While boys' schools achieve worse GCSE results than both girls' schools and co-educational schools, MFL is something of an anomaly in the curriculum. It is one of the few subjects in which single-sex educated boys do better than their peers in mixed schools. This suggests that there may be something about the single-sex environment that renders it more conducive to boys learning languages effectively.

Pupils' responses to being taught in single-sex groups

The findings suggest that there are far more differences between the responses of individual groups, regardless of their gender, than between boys and girls. Gender differences were, however, apparent in the responses of those boys and girls who were interviewed before they were placed in single-sex groups. While the girls' expectations were often very positive, the boys' apprehension was considerably more pronounced:

> *(Boys, Year 8)*
> AB: How did you feel when you were told that you were going to be taught in an all-boys' group next year?
> S: I thought it was a bad idea, 'cos mixing all the boys from all the other classes ... for the teacher it may be harder to control. We'll all talk ...
> M: I think it will be a disaster.
> AB: Why?
> M: Because all boys together ...
> D: We're loud.
> M: We're lively and that. It's bad enough in PE.
> C: It is.
> S: And I think the forms that we're mixing with and some of the people ...

These boys are, it seems, unanimous in their rejection of the idea for the following two reasons: their own poor behaviour and the fear of being in a group without their friends.

Those girls who did express some reluctance tended to relate this to a notion of their right, and need, to work alongside the opposite sex:

> *(Girl, Year 8)*:
> R: Well, I think it's an all right idea, but I think you need to work with boys because all our life we'll have to at some point. We can't just stay away from them ...

This reservation was expressed much more often by girls than boys and can probably be ascribed to girls' greater awareness of equal opportunities issues. Like the girls in other studies, a number voiced strong objections to single-sex setting on the grounds that it was 'sexist'. Their unclear understanding of this term, demonstrated in interviews, suggests that their usage of it is often borrowed from adult vocabulary and used with only limited understanding of its implications.

Behaviour

Criticism of boys' behaviour in mixed groups, the principal reason behind many girls' preference for single-sex groups and for their largely positive expectations, was frequently voiced in interviews, even when girls were unimpressed by the quality of teaching in their new classes:

(Year 7):
L: . . . boys just laugh if you get it wrong and they take the mickey out of you.
R: Lads are immature. They'll just sit there and somebody will say something and they giggle and mess about.

(Year 8):
R: The boys just butt in.
V: And they laugh as well. If you don't know it, it's horrible.

(Year 9):
C: We talk more . . . there's no one laughing at you.

While boys often claimed to be distracted by girls, they were generally far less likely to express direct criticism of girls' behaviour, other than, occasionally, to mention their chattiness in class. One of the reasons cited by a number of boys for not liking single-sex groups was that girls offered them assistance in mixed groups:

(Year 10): [Girls] help us with our work because they usually know more.

(Year 7): And they've got nice work. You can just, like, borrow . . . If a girl's next to us we can concentrate more. Wow, nice work, mind if I copy it?

The few girls who mentioned boys helping them related this specifically to boys' greater confidence in speaking. It was not always clear whether girls appreciated this because they were encouraged by the boys' example to contribute more themselves, or whether it was because they felt relieved that they would not be called upon to contribute as much in class since they could hide behind the boys' loquaciousness.

Pupil confidence

Large numbers of boys and girls mentioned feeling more confident in a single-sex group. While girls often recognized that boys dominated mixed classes, causing them to adopt a more passive role in the group, the boys often acknowledged that in a mixed group they were under 'pressure to impress' (Year 8 boy).

Friends

Pupils also perceived the benefits of being in a class with friends of the same sex. Boys often felt that this produced a more relaxed atmosphere but did not, like the girls, refer frequently to the mutual support offered by the group:

> *(Girl, Year 9)*: It's brilliant ... if you're stuck you can ask them a question if Miss is busy.

> *(Girl, Year 10)*: Our classroom's like a close-knit community. That's how it is ... It's just all one big 'sister' group. I don't see Miss as my teacher, I see her like a big sister.

Close relationships of the kind described above were often noted as a striking feature of all-girls' groups but only rarely observed in boys' groups.

Reasons for disliking single-sex groups

The most frequently cited reason for boys' and girls' dislike of the single-sex setting relates to the social disadvantages of not being with the opposite sex. Pupils who did not enjoy being in a single-sex class described 'having a laugh' in a mixed group, or commented on language learning being more enjoyable or fun in the company of the opposite sex. These pupils disliked single-sex setting because it was 'boring'.

The second most frequently cited reason among boys refers to criticism of their own sex. Boys often mentioned the noisiness of their group and to boys 'messing about':

(Year 10): . . . all boys tend to mess about more, I think.

(Year 7): You can't learn much in an all-boys' group because you're always talking . . .

Only a minority of girls criticized their own sex, describing the class as 'too quiet' and desiring the 'excitement' and entertainment offered by a mixed one. Some of these girls missed the male 'jesters' present in the mixed classroom and subscribed to the following view of boys' function in mixed groups:

(Mixed class, Year 10): . . . it would be boring without the odd fool.

Pupils in the study appear more convinced that a single-sex grouping is conducive to hard work than that it is enjoyable. In interviews, girls appeared to be much more convinced than boys that their work was benefiting from the new grouping. Among boys there were stark contrasts between the responses of those taught in single-sex groups:

(Year 10): It's a lot quieter. You get down to your work a lot quicker.

(Year 9): . . .most of the class is messing about and the teacher is shouting at them, and they're not getting their work done.

(Year 8): People concentrate more . . . You do more work.

These differences seem largely related to the teacher's management of the group. Those boys who claimed that they were not working as hard usually described the uncontrolled 'messing about' of their peers. Observation of the three groups, to whom the three boys quoted above belonged, suggested that the creation of an effective working environment in an all-boys' group is heavily dependent on the ability of the teacher to control the group. In those groups where teachers appeared to exercise strict control over behaviour, boys often mentioned working together as a team. In less well-disciplined groups fragmentation seemed to ensue, with boys allying themselves with small splinter groups between whom there was often confrontation.

The sex of the teacher

Several boys in interviews described how female teachers experienced greater problems with discipline in all-boys' groups than male teachers:

(Boy, Year 9): [I think there's a difference] 'cos all the boys think, 'Oh, she's female and she won't shout that much'. That's why they're naughty ...

(Boy, Year 10): It would be better if we had a male teacher ... because there isn't really that much respect for the teacher. It's hard for a female teacher to teach them.

Such comments reflect many female teachers' own accounts of the difficulties experienced by female teachers of boys' groups.

Pupils of both sexes who are taught in single-sex groups appear more convinced than their peers in mixed groups of the benefits of being taught by a teacher of the same sex as themselves. A few boys in interviews recognized that it was an advantage to be taught by a male teacher in an all-boys' group since he was more likely to be able to engage their interest than a female teacher:

(Boy, Year 8): It is different with Mr F because when we've finished our work we just read French comics, and they're Mr F's, he brings them in. ... I don't think Ms T would bring in comics like Superheroes and that ...

Several girls also found that a female teacher was more able to relate to them. While the boys' appreciation of a male teacher often tended to be based on perceived common interests, the girls' appreciation appeared to be more of the teacher's ability to empathize with them:

(Girl, Year 9): I think it's better for the girls being taught by a female teacher 'cos she understands you a bit more.

(Girl, Year 10): I think we prefer it with a woman teacher. She seems easy to relate to.

There was general uncertainty among teachers about the role played by their own gender in the effectiveness of the single-sex grouping. Some teachers felt more at ease with their groups because they were of the same sex:

(Teacher of Year 9 girls): I talk to [the girls] in a way that I probably wouldn't talk to the boys, and I don't know why. I'm just a lot more comfortable with them; I'm uncomfortable with the boys. I'm more relaxed with the girls.

(Teacher of Year 9 boys): It probably makes a difference being a male teacher. It's definitely an advantage. I had a parent come up to me last night demanding that her son is in my class next year, saying that he feels secure with me.

One male teacher of Year 10 boys referred specifically to the bonding process that took place in the group:

... there has been this bonding thing. At times I have felt there's been a father–like relationship. 40-50 per cent of them are from one-parent families. I present an alternative role model. They know that I'm a dad, I'm successful in my career, I play football.

A considerable number of teachers experienced particular problems with classes of the opposite sex. Of the three boys' groups that were observed, one, taught by the only female teacher of the three, was less than effective. The few male teachers of girls' groups in the study also encountered some problems with poor behaviour. These were particularly noticeable with older classes of girls, such as a Year 9 lower ability girls' class taught by a young male teacher who attributed to them a 'building-site mentality'. On the one occasion when the group was observed, this description appeared justified by the pupils' use of sexual innuendo that accompanied a French lesson on the theme of the body.

The effects of single-sex grouping on pupils' attitudes to modern foreign languages

The data suggest that single-sex grouping is only one of many variables that affect pupils' attitudes to modern languages, and many pupils in interviews found it difficult to assess the impact of the new grouping. Many pupils claimed to perceive no difference in their attitude and often, when pupils noticed a change in their attitude to languages from year to year, they were unable to attribute it to any distinct feature. When encouraged to elaborate, however, they most often named the teacher and their teaching style as the most important affective variables. A number went on to concede that they were probably influenced by a combination of the teacher and grouping variables. In one school which had also introduced ability setting alongside single-sex grouping, boys placed in higher ability groups also commented on the importance of being set by ability.

A number of pupils in a range of classes commented on the appropriateness of single-sex setting for a subject which incorporates inherent gender divides. They saw the single-sex grouping as an opportunity to avoid wasting time learning language associated with the opposite sex which, they thought, they would not need to employ:

(Girl, Year 7): Learning French in an all-girls' group is a good idea because there are different ways of spelling between boys and girls and it would have taken a long time to write out everything twice.

(Boy, Year 9): I think there's a need for [single-sex teaching] in French and German because you've got different words for feminine and masculine. The stuff that we're taught is mostly masculine ... We get told the feminine stuff and we put it down in our vocabulary book, but we don't use it.

Teachers' perceptions of girls' performance in single-sex groups

The majority of teachers expressed strong conviction that girls may benefit academically from being taught in a single-sex class.

The principal benefit for girls was perceived as their release from the overbearing influence of vociferous, dominant boys, the deciding factor in one school's initial decision to segregate. Girls' progress was often associated with their increased confidence. This new-found assertiveness was frequently mentioned in interviews:

(Teacher of Year 9 girls): The able girls have become very assertive. In speaking they're not shy any more and there's almost a boy element of competing for the limelight. Most of them are considered by the rest of the staff to be shy, retiring violets.

(Teacher of Year 7 girls): I think they felt quite safe in their group. They were used to each other and there wasn't one of them that didn't want to speak. Whereas I notice in my mixed Year 7 class there are a few that you don't hear, who will not willingly put their hand up, and it's the same few who always put their hand up.

The transition from reticence to assertiveness did not generally occur as a matter of course. In the early stages of the initiative, girls' teachers often described the difficulty they encountered in encouraging girls to speak out. In a number of cases individual 'boy substitutes' emerged who attempted to monopolize the teacher's attention and were readily accepted in this role by their peers who were accustomed to being 'swamped' by male classmates. When teachers deliberately applied strategies to counter this tendency, employing more pair- and group-work and encouraging them, in some cases, to view 'boyish' behaviours such as shouting as acceptable, girls' self-confidence seemed to flourish. Those teachers who did not appear to apply such measures found themselves frustrated by girls' passivity:

(Teacher of Year 9): They're extremely quiet, they don't give anything back at all, very unreceptive ... They still don't like speaking out in class, you have to drag things out of them.

This teacher's attitude to the group may well have been influenced by her conviction, expressed in an interview, that boys were 'a lot more fun'. She was also the only teacher to disagree with the questionnaire suggestion that 'Girls may learn languages better in single-sex groups'. Seen in the context of the claim from one of her pupils that speaking in her class was embarrassing, this case suggests that the improved performance of girls, and particularly their greater self-confidence, is not automatically guaranteed by the establishment of an all-girls' group. It would appear to be largely dependent on the teacher's attitude to the group, which inevitably informs their ability to create both sound working relationships with the pupils and a non-threatening working environment.

Teachers' perceptions of boys' performance in single-sex groups

The majority of teachers were aware that teaching an all-boys' group represented a rather more intense experience than teaching an all-girls' or mixed group. They mentioned boys' lack of self-control and the unpredictability of their behaviour as particular problems. A few teachers felt that the polarity and intensity of boys' emotions could offer certain advantages; they described how relationships with boys were likely to be more clear-cut, and related the passion with which their pupils had engaged with some topics.

Teachers' perceptions of the benefits derived by boys from the grouping were diverse, as the following comments indicate. These were made by teachers of boys' groups within the same school, in response to the question of whether the single-sex grouping had been effective in terms of raising boys' achievement:

Ms C, teacher of higher ability pupils: With that group, no. Purely because there are some individuals in the group who are not capable of working by themselves, who need to have someone else in the group who will lead for them, almost. There are some quite strong characters who've made the group disruptive.

Ms M, teacher of lower ability pupils: I don't know ... My boys have probably achieved what they would have produced anyway. I don't feel it's improved what they have achieved.

Mr R, teacher of higher ability pupils: Very much so. In terms of discipline and achievement I feel that they've learned a lot.

In comparison with girls' groups, all-boys' groups, it seems, are less likely to represent a clear-cut and short-term formula for improving pupil performance.

What are the potential advantages of teaching single-sex groups?

All of the teachers in this study agreed with the questionnaire suggestion that 'Boys and girls have different learning styles' and a number of them recognized the potential benefits of single-sex grouping in allowing them to tailor their teaching styles to meet the common needs and learning styles of the group:

(Teacher of Year 7/8): It's allowed me to look at the strengths and weaknesses of the boys much more clearly and, as a result, I've targeted areas which I feel they need to do more work on.

Several teachers used this opportunity to address boys' weaknesses, including organizational, social and writing skills, while teachers of girls' groups focused their attention on encouraging girls to become more assertive and adventurous in class.

A large number of teachers endorsed the suggestion that boys in boys' groups may become less aware of the image they convey to their peers than in mixed groups, where the presence of girls may heighten their sensitivity to the need to conform to fashionable, anti-academic male stereotypes. Several teachers referred to both boys and girls appearing more 'relaxed' and able to ask questions, in the boys' case without fear of being teased for demonstrating an interest in work. Single-sex groups were sometimes seen as giving the pupils the opportunity to explore their interests more freely since their questions often focused not on the specific linguistic area being taught but on broader issues related to languages. In one school, higher ability Year 9 girls were keen to discuss the development of different languages, and the implications of learning two languages, while the parallel boys demanded much more detailed explanations of grammatical points than the teacher had anticipated.

The most striking feature of the teacher perceptions collected in this research is the broad diversity of opinion. While these teachers are, it seems, agreed on a principal argument for establishing single-sex groups – boys' and girls' differential learning styles – they are by no means unified in their views on the success of such initiatives.

The greatest differences in opinion are to be found among teachers of boys' groups. While the majority of girls' teachers agree that the setting is effective, particularly in terms of improving girls' assertiveness and speaking skills, perceptions of boys' performance in single-sex groups vary widely. An improvement in boys' performance in these groups seems to be dependent on a complex chemistry of independent variables including ability setting, class size, the teaching style employed and, most importantly, the relationship with the teacher. Other factors highlighted by teachers, but not discussed in detail here, may comprise pupils' awareness of the 'novelty value' of such groups; the timetabling of language lessons; and the turn-over of staff in language departments.

There is a clear dividing line between those boys' groups which are effective and those which are not. The teachers of all-boys' groups were ostensibly subject to extremes of experience. In those cases where the setting was judged effective, teachers fostered a close relationship with their pupils and saw improvements in targeted weak areas such as social and organizational skills and writing. In unsuccessful classes teachers experienced a deterioration in discipline which forced them to deliver unstimulating lessons structured to maximize control.

The most positive attitudes among boys were expressed by younger boys of higher ability who were being taught by a teacher, male or female, who felt comfortable teaching boys and who was implementing carefully planned strategies to engage boys' interest. The appropriate pairing of teachers with classes seems to be a key factor in determining the effectiveness of single-sex grouping. Single-sex groups are most effective when they allow teachers to practise a teaching style that is inevitably informed by their age, sex and experience, with which they and their pupils are comfortable.

Which other factors affect pupils' performance?

Being a foreign native speaker

The teacher of one Year 8 boys' group found that his pupils were considerably more relaxed in his all-boys' group, although observation and his own comments suggested that the ease of his relationship with the class was also attributable to his status as a foreigner learning English:

> ...they were very shy in the beginning. So I said, 'Look, I make mistakes learning English, and you make mistakes in French. You teach me English, and I'll teach you French.' So we are on the same level, but I have the reins of the whole thing. Sometimes I do it deliberately, to shock them, and they say, 'Sir! You can't say that!' And I say, 'Well, I don't know, I'm a poor foreigner.' And they say, 'You're doing well, Sir, you're doing well.' I take advantage of that.

This teacher's deliberate exploitation of his uncertain knowledge of English also involved his mock-naive emulation of the boys' colloquial English, an action which also appeared to enhance his relationship with them. It is possible that boys' embarrassment in speaking a foreign language may be reduced when their teacher exploits the fact that he is genuinely sharing their experience of learning a foreign language. Exploiting one's 'foreignness' can therefore be advantageous!

Setting by ability

Pupils in this research seemed to attach considerable importance to learning a modern language in a group set by ability. The pupils in one particular school appeared to appreciate this most, perhaps because the single-sex sets had also, for the first time in modern languages, taken into account pupils' ability. Boys felt that this was part of the reason why they were now working better:

(Year 9):

D: I suppose it's top set as well, isn't it? So there's more people around me who want to get on with their work, so I get on with my work as well.

A: [I'm working] better, I think, because we're in sets as
          well. So everyone's more at the same level.

Some boys also felt that weaker boys were ridiculed in mixed
ability sets. For a number of teachers, ability setting was perceived
to play as important a role as single-sex grouping in influencing
pupils' performance. Concerns that mixed ability setting was not
conducive to language learning were voiced in two of the three
schools with current or recent experience of teaching mixed
ability groups. Teachers in a school where all pupils in Year 7
were taught in mixed ability single-sex groups, were particularly
critical of the inappropriateness of mixed ability setting in a
subject which is so unlike others:

Ms K: There are some pupils who have special needs who
would really benefit from having the whole lesson geared
towards them, but you can't do that when you've got a big
group in the middle and a few at the top. In other subjects you
can differentiate the task easier ... with French at this level, it's
so teacher-centred. You've got to aim just at the middle.

Ms M: Unless you have some specific grouping, some top sets,
you cannot stretch the better able ones. I always feel very guilty
that those who want to go on to 'A' level do not get the full
grammatical input that they need.

In contrast, in the school where pupils were set by gender and,
for the first time, by ability, teachers were delighted by the new
grouping and most were unable to decide which innovation –
ability or single-sex setting – had been more influential in raising
pupil achievement. Most seemed to endorse the Head of
Department's verdict that:

Doing both is more powerful than doing one or doing the
other ...

Class size
Boys, girls and teachers all agree that smaller classes are more
important for MFL than for other subjects. Year 10 girls in one
school qualified their preference for smaller classes by referring to
the comparative difficulty of French:

G: Small classes [are important].

K: 'Cos we have to wait half an hour for Ms X to see our work, and it's harder for her. You end up having a go at her.

AB: How many are in the group?

K: 25–30.

G: In science we've got bigger classes than that.

D: But science is all in English. French is a lot harder than that. You need a lot more of the teacher's attention really.

Perceptive comments such as this clearly illustrate pupils' understanding of how the learning environment may influence their achievements in what is perceived to be a difficult subject.

Teachers were also acutely aware of the influence of pupil numbers. In interviews some teachers of boys' groups attributed some of the success of the grouping to the opportunity it had given them to reduce the size of the class:

(Teacher of Year 10): Some of these boys would have sunk completely in larger groups – we had the benefit also of being a small group . . .

In a number of schools the creation of single-sex classes had resulted in larger than average groups. While large classes of girls, and higher ability boys, did not seem to create insurmountable problems, large classes of lower or mixed ability boys were often perceived as less manageable than large mixed-sex groups. Thus 32 higher ability boys in one school presented scarcely any disciplinary problems, in stark contrast to the 26 lower ability boys in a second and the 28 mixed ability boys in a third. Class size was frequently regarded by teachers as a key variable in distinguishing one class from another, as one teacher found in comparing her ill-disciplined Year 7 boys' group of 28 with her Year 8 group:

(Year 7/8, mixed ability): My Year 8 boys' group has only got about twenty at the most. And they are actually a pleasure to teach, that group. But that's probably to do with the numbers . . . they're a much smaller group.

Timetabling

Boys, more often than girls, frequently argue that because languages is a more difficult subject that demands concentration it should be taught when boys are mentally alert – in the morning, rather than after the lunchtime football match. Such views reinforce those frequently expressed by teachers who recognize the importance of timetabling foreign language classes appropriately. The point was first raised, unprompted, by a boy in Year 8 who recognized that afternoon timetabling of French lessons had an effect on his ability to learn:

> I don't mind French, I think it's a good subject and we should be taught it, but the thing I don't like is somehow, every time I do French it's always in the afternoon, and I'm always tired in the afternoon. I'd rather just have a subject what I can do easily, and I find French not hard, but you have to, like, concentrate. I'd rather have it in the morning, when I'm fresh.

Perceptive pupils seem to recognize that the inherent difficulty of learning a foreign language needs to be addressed in the timetable.

(Year 8 boys):

M: After lunch we're too tired to learn.

AB: Is that the same for all subjects?

G: No, just for a foreign language. You need to pay more attention, don't you?

M: More than in other subjects, because if you miss something . . .

8 Looking to the future

The challenge of motivating pupils to succeed in languages should not be underestimated. The list below comprises an array of strategies that could be implemented by you in this marathon bid to raise boys' achievement. These range from strategies on the starting line that are easy to implement to more ambitious strategies on the finish- line.

The majority of MFL teachers testify that the subject is more difficult to teach than other subjects, not least because its multi-skill content can easily create problems with behaviour management. This is obviously a significant concern for MFL teachers, who perhaps consequently need to be better managers of pupils' behaviour than their colleagues. *Getting the Buggers to Behave* (Continuum, 2001) is worth reading for its abundance of practical tips.

It is extremely important that you do not feel that you are running the MFL marathon alone. Sharing strategies and resources with colleagues and observing each others' lessons can be extremely productive. Membership of the Association for Language Learning (ALL) can also keep you up-to-date with the latest developments in language teaching and enable you to have your say in policy. Group membership is now available for MFL departments so that subscription can come out of the school budget rather than your own pocket.

We should be wary of assuming that boys will underachieve in MFL as a matter of course. Our goal should be to differentiate appropriately, allowing both boys and girls to realize their potential without being held back by restricting stereotypical views of what is suitable for boys and girls. While the research from which this book originated focused on boys' learning styles, what is striking about the data collected from schools is that differences between boys and girls are, surprisingly, only marginal. Differences in motivation emerge particularly at Key Stage 4 when boys begin to realize that they are not going to use their languages, the subject is of limited relevance to their futures, and that games – the only redeeming feature of lessons for many boys – give way to recycling topics visited at Key Stage 3. A pedagogy for boys may be unfeasible, or unnecessary, but what is clear is that boys are generally more sensitive to poor teaching than girls who may naturally be more at ease with language-based subjects.

This is an exciting, albeit equally unnerving, time for teachers of Modern Foreign Languages. Recent policy, shifting the focus of learning from Key Stage 4 to Key Stage 2, means that many teachers will have to re-examine and adapt their pedagogy in order both to accommodate younger learners and to ensure that Key Stage 3 learners are adequately motivated to continue their studies. It is worth remembering that no matter how many new initiatives teachers implement, or have imposed upon them, they ultimately play the key role in their pupils' motivation and achievement. The pupils themselves always attribute their enjoyment of languages to a good teacher:

> *(Boy, Year 10)*: It's actually because of the teacher. Years 7, 8 and 9 I found a bit boring because you just had to sit down and shut up and listen. This year there's a bit of humour in it as well . . . We've got a good teacher.

> *(Year 8 boys)*:
> M: We've had more of a laugh [this year], he's funny. It's because of the teacher . . .
> G: He's a good teacher. Star teacher definitely. You have to have a good teacher.

> *(Year 10 boys)*
> AB: Do you think it's important being in an all-boys' group?
> C: No, I don't think it is.
> S: It's not really important. It's just the same as in other groups.
> C: It's the teacher that's most important. He's got to make the lessons enjoyable, or you just lose interest.

The Equal Opportunities MFL Marathon (A departmental action plan)

The starting line . . .

- Establish the scale of the problem. Compare boys' and girls' GCSE grades and boys' success rate in other subjects.

- 'Market research' in school. Identify boys' and girls' likes and dislikes and learning styles.

- Structured observation of colleagues to identify ways of successful interaction and boys' responses to learning tasks.

- Consult pupils on best ways to proceed.

- Make assessment criteria clear so that pupils know how to succeed with a piece of work.

- Give constructive advice in marking on how to improve.

- Use a structured approach, which is clear to the pupil, for termly schemes of work and for each lesson.

- Teach in small steps; give pupils regular experience of success.

- Extend use of rewards/commendations to acknowledge boys' contributions.

- Individual target-setting.

- Use assessment criteria which recognize boys' contributions (Is equal value attached to speaking/listening as writing?)

- Target specific learning skills, e.g. dictionary/predictive skills.

- Review profile and image of languages in school. Does the subject have a feminine image?

- Extra-curricular support for boys who are underachieving in comparison with other subjects.

- Work with IT department to develop a meaningful way of using IT in all year groups.

- Mentoring system – male sixth-formers?

- Demonstrate practical values of language learning through inviting male linguists from business/industry into lessons.

- Organize trips to the workplace, e.g. Rover, Peugeot, to show languages at work.

- Look at criteria for setting.

- Evaluate boys' and girls' perceptions of different languages and act on preferences.

- Share findings/strategies with neighbouring schools.

- Single-sex setting in the early stages? (Yrs 7/8/9).

. . . . *THE FINISHING LINE!*

Recommended reading

Gender and achievement

Barton, A. (1997) 'Boys' under-achievement in GCSE modern languages: reviewing the reasons' *Language Learning Journal*, 16, 11–16.

Bleach, K. (ed.) (1998) *Raising boys' achievement in schools*, Trentham Books.

Clark, A. and Millard, E. (eds) (1998) *Gender in the Secondary Curriculum*, Routledge (Chapter 2 on 'Resistant boys and modern languages').

Clark, A. (1998) *Gender on the agenda. Factors motivating boys and girls in MFLs*, CILT.

Cornforth, A. (ed.) (2000) *The Underachievement of Boys: Finding the Solutions*, Latchmere Press (tel. 020 639 7282). (Chapter 10 on strategies for raising boys' achievement in MFL by Amanda Barton, and a description by Nick Jones of his experience of teaching French to an all-boys' group.)

Head, J. (1999) *Understanding the Boys*, Falmer Press.

Noble, C. and Bradford, W. (2000) *Getting it right for Boys . . . and Girls*, Routledge.

Pickering, J. (1997) *Raising Boys' Achievement*, Network Educational Press.

MFL pedagogy and motivating pupils in MFL

Chambers, G. (ed.) (2000) *Reflections on Motivation*, CILT (Chapter 2 on Gender differences in pupils' perceptions of modern foreign languages by Amanda Barton).

Macaro, E. (2001) *Learning Strategies in Foreign and Second Language Classrooms*, Continuum.

Morgan, C. and Neil, P. (2001) *Teaching Modern Foreign Languages. A Handbook for Teachers*, Kogan Page.

Pachler, N. and Field, K. (2001, 2nd edn) *Learning to Teach Modern Foreign Languages in the Secondary School*, Routledge.

Pleuger, J. (2001) *How to Teach Modern Languages – and Survive!* Multilingual Matters.

Swarbrick, A. (ed.) (2002) *Teaching Modern Foreign Languages in Secondary Schools*, RoutledgeFalmer/Open University.

Ur, P. (1999) *A Course in Language Teaching*, Cambridge University Press.

The CILT Pathfinder series comprises books that are packed with practical tips and inexpensive.

Language Learning Journal, published by ALL, is sent to all members and contains articles on a range of pedagogical issues. The related language-specific journals, also sent to members, contain more practical ideas and worksheets for use in the classroom.

It is also worth consulting books on Teaching English as a Foreign Language, of which there are many. They contain an abundance of practical and effective strategies for effective teaching. Two examples are:

Baker, J. and Westrup, H. (2000) *The English Language Teacher's Handbook*, Continuum.

Baker, J. and Westrup, H. (2003) *Essential Speaking Skills*, Continuum.

Useful addresses

ALL (Association for Language Learning)
Head Office
150 Railway Terrace
Rugby
CV21 3HN
Tel: 01788 546443
email: *info@ALL-languages.org.uk*
www.ALL-languages.org.uk

AQA (Assessment and Qualifications Alliance)
Aldon House
39 Heald Grove
Rusholme
Manchester
M14 4PB
Tel: 01423 840015
www.mfl-s@aqa.org.uk

BECTA (formerly NCET) – for advice on how to use ICT in
MFL teaching
Millburn Hill Road
Science Park
Coventry
CV4 7JJ
Tel: 024 7641 6994
Fax: 024 7641 1418
email: *becta@becta.org.uk*

Camsoft UK (one of the biggest software manufacturers)
10 Wheatfield Close
Maidenhead
Berkshire
SL6 3PS
Tel: 01628 825206
Fax: 01628 820431
info@camsoftpartners.co.uk

CILT (Centre for Information on Language Teaching and Research)
20 Bedfordbury
Covent Garden
London WC2N 4LB
Tel: 020 7379 5101 ext. 248 for publications, 229 for training events and 020 7379 5110 for library and information services.
www.cilt.org.uk

Comenius Centre
Manchester College of Arts and Technology
City Centre Campus
Lower Hardman Street
Manchester
M3 3EK
Tel: 0161 953 2266
Fax: 0161 953 2259

Department for Education and Skills (DfES)
Sanctuary Buildings
Great Smith Street
London SW1P 3BT
Tel.: 020 7925 5000
Fax: 020 7925 6000
www.open.gov.uk/dfee/dfeehome.htm

Edexcel
Adamsway
Mansfield NG18 4LN
Tel: 01623 467467
Fax: 01623 450481
email: *enquiries@edexcel.org.uk*, *publications@mailin.co.uk*

GTC (General Teaching Council)
10 Greycoat Place
London SW1P 1SB
email: *info@gtce.org.uk*

Institute of Linguists
Saxon House
48 Southwark Street
London SE1 1UN
Tel: 020 7940 3100
Fax: 020 7354 0202

Mary Glasgow Magazines/Scholastic ELT
Commonwealth House
1–19 New Oxford Street
London WC1A 1NU
Tel: 020 7421 9050
Fax: 020 7421 9051

OCR
Oxford Cambridge and RSA Examinations
Mill Wharf
Mill Street
Birmingham B6 4BU
Tel: 01223 552662
Fax: 01223 552930
www.ocr.org.uk

Office for Standards in Education (Ofsted)
Alexandra House
29 Kingsway
London WC2B 6SE
Tel: 020 7421 6800
Fax: 020 7421 6707
http://www.open.gov.uk/ofsted/ofsted.htm

QCA (Qualifications and Curriculum Authority)
29 Bolton Street
London W1Y 7PD
Tel.: 020 7509 5555
email: info@qca.org.uk
www.qca.org.uk

Teacher Training Agency
Portland House
Stag Place
London SW1E 5TT
Tel.: 020 7925 3700
www.canteach.gov.uk

Index